00200

A Doctor's Personal Journey
through Breast Cancer

TAFFY A. ANDERSON, M.D.

MOODY PUBLISHERS
CHICAGO

All Scripture quotations, unless otherwise indicated, are taken from the King James Version.

Scripture quotations marked NIV are taken from the *Holy Bible, New International Version*. NIV®. Copyright © 1973, 1978, 1984 by International Bible Society. Used by permission of Zondervan. All rights reserved.

Scripture quotations marked KNKJV are taken from the *New King James Version*. Copyright © 1982 by Thomas Nelson, Inc. Used by permission. All rights reserved.

Cover Design: David Holmon
Interior Design: Ragont Design
Editor: Kathryn Hall

Library of Congress Cataloging-in-Publication Data

Anderson, Taffy A.
    Treasures in darkness : a doctor's personal journey through breast cancer / Taffy A. Anderson.
        p. cm.
    Includes bibliographical references.
  · ISBN-13: 978-0-8024-8250-1
    ISBN-10: 0-8024-8250-3
        1. Breast—Cancer—-Patients—Religious life. 2. Breast—Cancer—Religious aspects—Christianity. 3. Suffering—Religious aspects—Christianity. 4. Anderson, Taffy A. I. Title.

BV4910.33.A53 2007
248.8'619699490092—dc22
[B]
                        2007003115

1 3 5 7 9 10 8 6 4 2

Printed in the United States of America

TO JESUS CHRIST, MY LORD AND
SAVIOR, TO WHOM I BELONG.

CONTENTS

Foreword   9

Acknowledgments   11

Introduction   15

CHAPTER 1:
   When a Sibling Is Diagnosed: "Shereene"   23

CHAPTER 2:
   The Denial: And How I Met "a Rock"   43

CHAPTER 3:
   The Diagnosis: "No, Not Me!"   57

CHAPTER 4:
   The Biopsy and Treatment Plan: "Okay, Maybe Me"   75

CHAPTER 5:
   Chemotherapy: "The Perfect Storm"   93

CHAPTER 6:
   Mastectomy: "Okay, I Surrender"   109

CHAPTER 7:
   Radiation Therapy: "It's Almost Over"   121

CHAPTER 8:
   Recovery Phase: "Oh, No, Not Marie!"   129

CHAPTER 9:
   Reconstruction: "I'm a New Creation"   143

CHAPTER 10:
   Healing Phase: "It's All about a Broken Leg"   149

Conclusion: Secrets and Treasures   165

Glossary   175

Afterword   181

FOREWORD

BY ESTHER SAWYER

*"And I will give [you] the treasures of
darkness, and hidden riches of secret places . . ."*
(ISAIAH 45:3)

I must confess. I never really understood what this Scripture meant until I read the following tremendous testimony of adversity leading to intimacy with God. I did not even understand that there were treasures in darkness and riches in secret places. After all, I pondered, you would need light to see treasures. And aren't secret places meant to be kept secret?

What an illumination of Isaiah 45:3 Dr. Taffy Anderson provides in this personal, easy-to-read account of one of the darkest times in her life. She lays before us—from beginning to end—the physical, emotional, psychological, and spiritual ups and downs of the excruciating process that the Lord took her through to accomplish His end. She does not conceal from us her human side: the questions, the anxiety, and her struggle during this process. Rather, Dr. Anderson uncovers for us the answers, the reassurance, and the ultimate deliverance that only her God, Jesus the Christ, could give.

Whether you're a fellow breast cancer survivor or patient; whether a Christian leader or layperson; and regardless of occupation, race, age, or even gender, this compelling view into the life and ominous season of a wife, first lady (of her church), and successful medical doctor will cause us all to realize—no matter who we are—that God is a God of purpose. We will discover through following her gripping journey that God desires to fully reveal Himself to us and make known His intentions for our lives, so that we would know Him and that He would receive all the glory.

Truly, God must be pleased that my doctor, my friend, and my godly example Taffy chose to share with us the treasures and secrets that He specifically and lovingly showed to her. I am convinced they were not just intended for her, but for us all. As we unwrap the secrets and draw from Taffy's story, we can begin to apply these priceless treasures to our own lives, so that we too may say with Paul, *"That I may know him, and the power of his resurrection, and the fellowship of his sufferings, being made conformable unto his death"* (Philippians 3:10).

◆
ACKNOWLEDGMENTS

There are so many people whom God placed in my path to help me through my journey with breast cancer. My husband was a rock of physical comfort that I constantly needed to help me see God's unfailing hand every time I had doubts. My mother was also a rock; I appreciated her endless love and support with the preparing of meals, the cleaning of my house, the washing of my clothes, and so on. Her very presence was like the stretched-out hand of God as she served me unselfishly—in spite of my less-than-perfect behavior.

My faithful and loving sisters proved to be there for me, providing warmth and emotional support, along with my dear brothers, who would visit or call me throughout my illness.

Although my dad could not physically be with me, I knew he was praying for me because he would tell me when I spoke with him. All of my nieces and nephews, whom I love so dearly and are like the children I never had, showered me with the prayers, love, and support that any auntie could ever want to have. To not only my immediate family, but my extended family as well, including my aunts, uncles, and cousins who visited me throughout my illness and comforted me with phone calls, I want to say I love you and thank you.

My mother-in-law and my father-in-law, Rev. Roland H. Anderson I, prayed with my husband and me on several occasions. He also put up with my many moods during this time as he helped to redecorate my home. Based on my mood, I would change the color of paint in my bathroom at a whim's notice. He was so kind and patient with me and never said a word; he just kept making trips to the paint store.

My niece Carla has become an advocate for breast cancer and has participated in several breast cancer walks. And my niece Dionna has donated some of her fashion design proceeds to the American Cancer Society. My nephews, John and JR, Shereene's sons, bravely experienced their mother and two aunts as we battled breast cancer within a few years of one another. By joining a fund-raising walk, John is so concerned about finding a cure for the disease; he was the first in my family to raise money for breast cancer research. However, shortly before the walk, he injured his leg and could not participate in the event, but he did raise a good sum of money; he remains a research advocate today. These are just a few of the things my relatives have done to help the fight for a breast cancer cure.

ACKNOWLEDGMENTS

I remember when Sister Melvenna Santiago, our women's ministry director, bought breast cancer pins for the ladies in our church; they are still wearing them five years later. I will never be able to thank or repay my entire church family, including the deacons, deaconesses, missionaries, Sunday school members, the women's fellowship, and pastors' aides who prayed night and day for me. I appreciate all of my sisters in Christ throughout my church who just gave me so much love and encouragement. They even embraced my mother and cared for her during the time she stayed with me. In fact, I have a lot of spiritual mothers in my church who ministered to me during this time, and two of them even reached out to my mother to comfort her during both Marie's illness and my own; they have become her best friends to this very day.

For their loving prayers, I want to truly thank all the local churches in the cities of Pottstown and Philadelphia, in the surrounding areas, and those as far away as California. I am eternally grateful for the many pastors, some of whom I know and others whom I don't know, who held my name before the Father daily. There may be others, but through my chemotherapy treatments, I could not remember them all—you know who you are, and I want to thank you as well.

There were scores of patients who called me periodically and kept in touch. God used them to minister to me in such a delightful way; sometimes I was up and sometimes I was down, but they all loved me anyway. For this I was blessed. My lifelong friends Barb, Esther, Joni, and Jean put up with me throughout my illness and are still the best friends that a former breast cancer patient could ever have. And again I am blessed.

Finally, I could not end this section without thanking all the people who helped to make this happen. In particular, to Cynthia Ballenger, who painstakingly worked with me throughout the course of my writing and was the coordinator for the entire book, I want to express my deep appreciation. For all the people who worked on the manuscript, including Celeste McGhee, Dr. William L. Banks, Minister Thomas Strode, Pam Pugh, and Kathryn Hall, who served as editor for my manuscript, I want to thank you for your patience and the efforts you put forth to help me accomplish this goal. And last, but not least, I would like to express my gratitude to all the people at Lift Every Voice and Moody Publishers for their generous support.

INTRODUCTION

Breast cancer is one of the leading causes of cancer deaths in women. The chance of a woman developing breast cancer in her lifetime is one out of eight according to the latest statistics from the American Cancer Society. It was also estimated that in the year 2006, 212,920 women would develop invasive breast cancer, and 40,970 would ultimately die from the disease.[1] Several prominent people with whom you are familiar have developed breast cancer in their lives, including the former first ladies Betty Ford and Nancy Reagan, as well as celebrities Diahann Carroll and Sheryl Crow. Singer/actress Olivia Newton-John has also courageously shared her story. There are numerous others who are not willing to openly disclose the details of the emotional journey they undertook, but they too are important and cannot be forgotten.

By having breast cancer, you automatically join the "sisterhood" in which you share a special link with other breast cancer survivors. In this sisterhood, we offer our stories of how we made it through and provide emotional support and encouragement to other sisters in their struggles. You don't get to choose to be a part of the sisterhood—it just happens—because once someone finds out you are a breast cancer survivor, you are called upon to offer support to other women. Sometimes women desire to remain anonymous in the sisterhood, and that is understandable, but know that we can all draw strength from the common bond that keeps us closely knit together.

Why women get breast cancer, we really do not know. It may be multifactorial; that is, a combination of hormonal, genetic, environmental, and even stress-related factors. Regardless of its cause, it is one of the most feared and dreaded diseases a woman can face in her lifetime. Perhaps breast cancer is so feared among women because it has such an emotional and physical impact on our lives. Other cancers may have equally devastating effects; I'm certainly not implying that people with other forms of cancer do not have emotional and physical implications as well. But with breast cancer I have observed such emotional changes in the women struck with this disease, and I believe it is because it deeply touches a woman at one of the core aspects of what she represents—her femininity.

The physical aspect is easy to understand because the physical body will go through many changes, and the subsequent treatments will alter one's appearance. But coping with the physical directly leads to the emotional changes that a woman undergoes. This is because breast cancer affects a part of the female body that is very visible and makes us strikingly different from men. A woman's breasts represent a part of her sexuality, even though we don't like to admit it and we think we are far above that kind of thinking.

It was not until I had to have my breasts removed that I realized the extremely emotional aspect of this disease. If you don't believe it is emotional, then sit one day in the chemotherapy room with women receiving their treatments and watch the tears on their faces as they hold out their arms to receive another chemotherapy injection. Or stand in the preoperative holding area and watch the women who are going for their mastectomies. I've seen their brave faces numerous times, and I've witnessed their sobbing. I've watched as they gripped their loved ones' hands before they proceeded down the corridor to the surgical suites—into the unknown. It's a highly emotional experience because when you emerge from surgery, whether it is a lumpectomy or mastectomy, you never look the same. A portion of your breast now lies on the pathology table, and you have a daily reminder of the cancer when you look in the mirror and see that a part of your breast is gone.

Not so with other female cancers. You cannot physically see or feel your ovaries or uterus before they are surgically removed. But with breast cancer it is different; you can see and feel the obvious changes in your body, and others can see it too. Therefore, it is emotional. If it were not emotional, then why do numerous women have breast-enhancing surgery to improve their appearances? Some of us would not have this kind of surgery, but many of us have thought about changing our looks; it goes along with being a woman.

Society tells us we are always supposed to be our best. If we are to do so, then we often feel that we must work on our appearance in order to improve upon ourselves. But with breast cancer, how are we to look better? How can you look your best when, after a mastectomy, you wear a breast prosthesis that may not even match the size of your other breast? How can you look better when your hair has fallen out from the chemotherapy treatments and you can hardly find a wig that matches your old hair? How can you look good when the chemotherapy treatments cause you to have difficulty walking and leave you with such fatigue that you can hardly put on your clothes? The commercials with beautiful women and their advertisements for beauty enhancements don't stop because you have breast cancer, although I wished they would.

On January 23, 2002, I was diagnosed with a disease most feared and dreaded by women. I too became an American Cancer Society's statistic by being diagnosed with stage three—or at least advanced stage two—invasive breast cancer. As a doctor in obstetrics and gynecology who is quite familiar with breast cancer, I never wanted to become *that* acquainted with the disease. I too became emotional when faced with the horror of this disease that I had seen in many of my patients.

As a breast cancer survivor, I needed to tell about my trial and my faith in God during a very physically and emotionally challenging time in my life. I call my experience a "journey through darkness." My story is about *going through* the darkness and not *staying in* the darkness—because, thanks be to

God, I eventually emerged victoriously.

Although I became a born-again Christian as a teenager, at age thirty-three I sincerely rededicated myself to the Lord and started seeking a deeper meaning to life. When I accepted the call to return to the Lord, I knew then that my life would be better. And for a while it was—until the storms of life hit. At the time of the diagnosis, horror, shock, and disbelief welled up in this overworked, tired, and worn-down doctor. Immediately, I surrendered to this horrendous disease. Breast cancer is the one illness that women don't like to talk about because of the shame and embarrassment that it brings. It carries a stigma with it, as if we brought it upon ourselves or it was caused by some curse from God. Through no desire of my own, I entered not only the "sisterhood" but what I also call a "state of darkness." A vague darkness descended over my mind and body, gripping me with fear about what the future held. In despair, I cried out to God, "What are You doing?" Then God assured me that He knew what He was doing.

Now that I have survived the darkness of breast cancer, I have written this book to tell about my victory in overcoming the big storm and several little ones in between. It is about how God delivered me by bringing me through the trial of breast cancer. It is also about the struggle with my confession of faith that finally anchored me in God. It is not about *removal* out of the storm, because that didn't happen, but about *going through* the storm and God's ultimate deliverance.

As a consequence of my experience, my story uncovers the treasures that I learned about God in the darkest state of my life. It is based on Isaiah 45:3 because one night while I was lying in bed very sick from chemotherapy, I asked God why I was going through this. As I was reading through the book of Isaiah, God gave me this Scripture: *"And I will give [you] the treasures of darkness, and hidden riches of secret places"* (Isaiah 45:3). This verse helped me to realize the things being learned while in the storm were about God. They then became treasures and riches that were coming out of the darkness; that is, secrets being revealed from God in the darkest period of my life.

Yes, breast cancer had struck. But the treasures I learned about God during this time caused me to develop a more personal and intimate relationship with Him than ever before. God was teaching me about His ways. Most of the time, treasures are to be held and not told, but because these treasures are so valuable, they need to be shared with other cancer patients and their families who are going through the storm and the darkness. They tell about the goodness of the Lord and invite others to look in and long for a personal relationship with Him.

This is not only a story about a doctor's journey, but a tale of three sisters and our plights together as we each walked through our breast cancer experiences. You will first hear about the trial of my eldest sister Shereene, the first to be diagnosed with the disease. Subsequently, you will hear about me, and then my sister Marie. Within a few months of completing my treatments, I learned that she too was diagnosed. This is about our survival and the lessons I learned through watching my sisters' battles with the disease as well.

This is a story about a doctor who became a patient, and not a very good one at that. It tells how this doctor had to learn how to depend on God because of the chemotherapy that caused her to be so sick. This doctor became the sickest cancer patient she had ever witnessed. This doctor experienced the same ill effects from the chemotherapy that she had given to her ovarian cancer patients. And because of this experience, she learned how to be a more attentive, compassionate, kind, and caring doctor to *all* patients.

As a doctor, I wish I could tell you that I made the profession look great as a model patient and how I sailed through the treatments, but I can't. I wish that I could tell you that this professed Christian doctor and pastor's wife was the model Christian, strong in the Lord, who made it through without any problems, but I can't. This is about a struggle *daily* with God and how I finally surrendered to His will. It was a day-to-day struggle—and sometimes an hourly struggle—to keep myself surrendered to Him so that He could bring forth fruit for His glory.

The intention of this book is also to inform you of the misconceptions I had as a physician about healing, and to give you the truth from God's Word. For some of you who are going through adversity right now, this book is intended to direct you to the Savior for His guiding light and the comfort that He has available to you right now—if you will let Him in. For those of you who have been through the storms of breast cancer, it is about true survival and how it was God who brought you through. For those who do not know the Savior, it is intended to direct you to accept His gift of salvation; and for those who do, it is to strengthen your walk with God. But most of all, it is to bring glory to God and give Him praise for who He is. As the Scripture says, *"By him therefore let us offer the sacrifice of praise to*

God continually, that is, the fruit of our lips giving thanks to his name" (Hebrews 13:15).

I now have a strong determination to continually give God thanks and praise—not only for who He is—but also for bringing me safely through the storm of breast cancer. In this book are written several treasures revealed to me by God during one of the darkest times of my life, the secrets of survival in a storm called breast cancer. The lessons I learned when looking back are lovingly shared with you.

—Taffy A. Anderson, M.D.

---

1. Copyright © 2006 American Cancer Society, Inc.
   http://www.cancer.org/docroot/CRI/CR_0.asp

WHEN A SIBLING IS DIAGNOSED: "SHEREENE"

My breast cancer journey did not just begin when I developed breast cancer in 2002. Although it physically started that year, emotionally, what I call my "cancer awakening or awareness," occurred long before I ever had breast cancer. It happened when my older sister was diagnosed in 1998. Among the sisters, Shereene was the first to be stricken with this disease.

As a practicing obstetrician/gynecologist (OB/GYN), I had diagnosed many breast masses in patients, but very few of them were cancerous. If I did suspect breast cancer, I referred these patients to a breast surgeon who took care of them and made the final diagnosis. Therefore, I had a transient relationship with most breast cancer patients in my practice. During my residency, I actively took care of ovarian and cervical cancer patients; however, after completion of the residency, this became true for the gynecological malignancies as well. I referred them to a gynecologic surgeon for their treatments. I may have made the diagnosis, but the patient was referred to a specialist who cared for them during their treatments.

So, aside from my residency training, I really did not get to see the full impact of the cancer disease in my patients. My residency consisted of four years of training in obstetrics and gynecology and included the cancer specialty in gynecologic oncology. This means that I had some training in taking care of ovarian, uterine, and cervical cancer patients. I even administered their chemotherapy treatments and assisted in their surgeries, but this was not enough experience to say that I understood the full impact that cancer had in their lives.

Throughout training at the university, we focused most of our energies on treatment protocols and helping the patients to survive. However, I will admit that we had some of the worst cases of cancer, and many of them did not survive. As a result, I only had a slight idea of the physical and emotional impact cancer had on patients—much less on their families. It wasn't until after my sister was diagnosed that I realized the emotional toll it took, not only on the patient but also on the family. You can say that I developed a real "cancer awareness" for patients and their families because of my experience with my sister.

When Shereene, my elder sister, developed breast cancer, I concerned myself with whether or not she was going to survive. I wondered, *How will she make it through her treatments? Will she lose her beautiful hair?* There were so many "what-ifs" that I could go on and on. Thank God, she did survive. But even after her treatments, I still worried about whether she would be okay in five or ten years. Belonging to a family with three sisters as close as we are made it an emotionally trying time for me to see what Shereene went through. I've never forgotten it. It would often replay in my mind how sick with nausea and vomiting she was from the chemotherapy treatments. Seeing her mastectomy scar, I wondered what she thought about the disfigurement. When we talked, she would often tell me how she battled the fatigue day in and day out. So I take you back to tell you her story, which is where I believe my story begins. It speaks of who I became after seeing my sister battle the disease.

It all began when I visited my sister in California to attend the high school graduation of my nephew John. Shereene told me she had a breast mass. I remember the trip distinctly because I had looked forward to being off work (from a busy schedule of delivering babies) and enjoying myself in California. I loved to visit Shereene and her husband, Jerry, because of the great relationship I had with them. Before my visits, I always anticipated that the weather was going to be sunny and warm. However, this trip was going to be quite different. After the commencement ceremony, we had a wonderful party in the backyard. The day was hot and the sky was clear without a cloud in sight. Everyone was in good spirits; the adults were talking and laughing, and the kids were running and jumping in the pool.

My sister was her usual self, full of laughter and lively talk. She was so glad to see her last child graduate from high school.

Shereene was a constant advocate of good health. She always maintained a size 8 dress size with a five-feet-nine-inch frame. She exercised regularly and continually looked like the picture of health whenever you saw her. She practiced good nutrition and had a strong influence on her husband and two sons as well. When I visited her, I would always sneak potato chips and cookies in the house to eat, much to her dislike.

Shereene did not want to alarm me when she picked me up from the airport, and she said nothing about her condition until the day after the graduation. As I was preparing that morning to return to Philadelphia, she told me she had a lump in her breast and wanted me to feel it. Being a practicing obstetrician/gynecologist since completing my residency in 1992, I was very familiar with breast disease. In fact, I graduated from Georgetown University Medical School, one of the nation's most prestigious schools. As a result, I had my pick of residency programs. I chose the University of Michigan because of its excellent training program, which included the study of breast diseases. It was one of the few programs that allowed residents to perform breast biopsies. So when my sister told me about her lump, I felt uneasy, but she is my sister, and I was confident that I could help her.

I sat down with Shereene and asked her some questions: "How long has the mass been there? When was your last mammogram?" She told me that the mass had been there about two months. When she had her last mammogram six months earlier, the results were negative. Based on this information, I felt assured that we were probably dealing with a benign condition.

Initially, it was strange examining my sister's breast, but at that moment I needed to put on a different hat—that of a doctor and not a sister. When I located the mass, the thought occurred to me that we could be dealing with a serious condition here. The mass was firm, approximately two centimeters in diameter, and not very mobile—all the signs of cancer. But I quickly reminded myself of her negative mammogram six months earlier. When she asked me what I thought, I considered her prior history of the negative mammogram only six months earlier and her long history of fibrocystic disease, a benign condition of the breast. I really thought it was benign, and I said so.

Almost 80 to 90 percent of women have fibrocystic changes, making it the most common finding in breast biopsies for women. This condition occurs more often than cancer.

Fibrocystic changes of the breast involve cystic areas in the breast (fluid) surrounded by fibrous tissue that is thick and firm. This causes nodularities in the breast which can result in breast lumps, pain, and tenderness. Fibrocystic changes of the breast have a tendency to be cyclic, meaning the symptoms usually come two to three weeks before the menstrual cycle begins and resolve by the time the cycle ends.

Shereene had two prior breast biopsies that showed fibrocystic changes that posed no risk for breast cancer. In spite of her prior history of the two benign breast masses, I told her to call the doctor and arrange for an exam that day. Being trained as a gynecologist, I was taught to immediately see patients who have breast masses. She called him right away, and he agreed to see her that morning. When the doctor examined her, he tried to aspirate the mass by drawing fluid from it to see if it was cystic. But when he could retrieve no fluid, he suspected it was solid and ordered a mammogram and breast ultrasound to be done right then.

However, I was certain it was benign, so Shereene dropped me off at the mall to return something before my flight departure. When my nephew picked me up, I knew there was a problem. He told me that they had taken Shereene for more testing, and I needed to come now. Of course, thinking the worse, I could not leave her if they were giving her a death sentence right there in the office. My mind wandered endlessly on the ride over to the hospital. *What if the mammogram was wrong? What will my family think? Is she going to die?* Finally, my thoughts settled just enough for me to look for my sister.

When I found Shereene in the radiology suite, she had a bewildered look on her face and said the radiologist was reviewing her films. I could not utter a word until I saw the films myself, so I frantically looked for the radiologist. Overhearing the radiologist talking about her on the phone, I rushed back to the radiology reading room and interrupted his lunch by introducing myself and asking, "What do you think?" He said it was mostly a solid mass, but since she had had a negative mammogram in the last six months, he was not sure. He recommended a biopsy.

The stream of fearful emotions that flooded my heart started to overwhelm me, but I had to hold it together to speak with Shereene. As a doctor I was trained to deliver bad news by suppressing my emotions until the patient left the room. This time would need to be somewhat different since this was my sister. I told Shereene that the mammogram showed the mass was mostly solid, but we still had hope because there were benign, noncancerous masses that were also solid. Surprisingly, she took the news very well and agreed to wait and see the breast surgeon before jumping to any conclusions. Having previously had two benign breast biopsies, she had traveled this road before.

Through her HMO insurance plan, Shereene was referred to a surgeon. This wonderful lady agreed to see her in two days. In the meantime, Shereene sent me home to Philadelphia. She told me that if it turned out to be cancer and she needed to have surgery, she would need me even more then. It was so unsettling to go home without knowing the outcome, but I realized that she was right, and I boarded a plane to return to Philadelphia. We agreed not to worry our mother by telling her, but Shereene did tell her husband. Two days later she had another aspiration performed by the surgeon, who told Shereene that she thought it was benign. Therefore, my sister and her husband went on vacation and then traveled on to Detroit to take her son John to college. The surgeon told Shereene to call her when she got back. Shereene and I both breathed a sigh of relief.

Upon her return from vacation, there was a note in the mail from the surgeon to call her immediately. Being very concerned, Shereene called the next day as soon as the office opened. To her surprise, the entire office was waiting for her call, and someone connected her with doctor right away. When the doctor spoke to Shereene, she said the aspirate showed some "atypical cells," and she wanted to do an open biopsy. Atypical cells are cells that look suspicious for cancer and need to be investigated immediately. An open biopsy is a procedure that involves removal of the suspicious tissue in the breast— either the total tissue or only a portion. My sister agreed and the open biopsy was scheduled for the next day. Because she had two prior biopsies and very dense breasts, Shereene was determined to reserve her reaction and wait for the final pathology report.

Although her prior two biopsies were negative for cancer, her gynecologist had recommended that she see an oncologist who would examine her breasts every six months for increased surveillance. So we knew that we could also call him if anything turned out to be cancerous. The next day Shereene had the biopsy. During the procedure, she noticed that the surgeon looked concerned when she hit a certain area of her breast and told Shereene she was going to go deeper. After the biopsy, she went home to wait for a call the following day. Now she was concerned, but she was still hoping for the best.

The following day I received the dreaded call: "Taff, come quickly!" The biopsy detected that it was cancer. A mastectomy had been scheduled for a couple of days later. She wanted to get this over with right away so that she could go on with her life. Shereene was shocked and in disbelief and wanted this cancer out of her body immediately; she wanted this over with. After I hung up the phone, my heart sank in disbelief too. There was only one cancer survivor in our family, and that was my aunt Rhena, whom we call "Auntie." She is my dad's sister and had developed breast cancer several years earlier. However, all the rest who had developed cancer had succumbed to the disease. My uncle—"Doc"—had died from prostate cancer, and my cousin Wilkie had died from breast cancer in her forties.

I called my friend from medical school who was now an oncologist at the Mayo Clinic and had a special interest in breast cancer. She was able to help by giving us the latest information on breast cancer. My friend reassured us that there had been great advances in breast cancer treatment since my medical school training. She stated that the research had come a long way and the survival rate was improving. This gave Shereene and her family hope, as well as me and the rest of our siblings. Before leaving for California to be with Shereene for her surgery, I had the opportunity to speak with her surgeon. She assured me that the mastectomy should be a cure, but Shereene would probably need postoperative chemotherapy. Feeling better with all the news I had been given about the advances in breast cancer, I boarded the plane with assurance that Shereene would be okay.

On the plane I was reminded of Auntie, who is one of my favorite aunts. She and her sisters are very close, and when they heard of Auntie's diagnosis, they all rallied around her and really supported her. Each sister came and spent time with Auntie after her surgery to help her through the tough time. They attended to her every need until she recovered. Auntie and her sisters have all been such great role models for my sisters and me in how they support and love each other. If one of them gets sick, they make regular visits or phone calls if they cannot be there. For years they have traveled together. And we have modeled this loving pattern within my family, embracing our nieces and nephews as well.

So when Shereene got breast cancer, Marie, my other sister,

and I knew exactly what to do. We had to rally around Shereene. We decided that I would go out for her surgery, and when I returned, Marie would go next. Mom took the news remarkably well. She has a firm spiritual foundation and really knows how to trust in the Lord. In fact, I've always said she was born for adversities and trials. It's not that she causes them, of course, but she knows how to weather the storms with God and to ride them out with the most awesomely positive outlook. Mom quit her job immediately and went to be with Shereene for as long as it took her daughter to get well, which was about six months.

Our family is very close. I am the youngest of seven, with four brothers and two sisters. All of us are close, especially the sisters. We are like triplets. We have a family tradition of frequently taking vacations together because we really enjoy being with each other. My sisters and I share many secrets and have even enjoyed living close to one another. When Marie and I both graduated from high school, we went west to live with Shereene. When Shereene was living in Spain, we also moved there temporarily to be with her. So when Shereene was diagnosed with cancer, it felt like we had it too; we both shared her pain.

When I returned to California in preparation for Shereene's surgery, we met with her surgeon to discuss the decision to perform a mastectomy as opposed to a lumpectomy. "I chose a mastectomy due to the size of the tumor, because I'm not sure with a lumpectomy I could get clear margins around the tumor and leave her much breast tissue," the surgeon explained. After seeing the mammogram, I agreed with her treatment plan.

Clear margins exist when the tumor is removed and the remaining breast tissue around the area where the cancer existed is free of cancer.

To make this happen, some of the good breast tissue is taken along with the cancerous tissue to be certain that no cancer is left behind. This is done during breast conservation; that is, a lumpectomy, where the tumor is removed along with some adjacent surrounding normal breast tissue. It assures the surgeon that he or she is getting clear margins so the remaining breast tissue is cancer free. Hopefully, this does not leave a large defect in the remaining breast tissue, but sometimes it does. Therefore, the surgeon may recommend a mastectomy to obtain clear margins and prevent leaving such a large defect in the breast. In Shereene's case, a mastectomy was better in order to ensure clear margins around the tumor.

We then discussed the possible reasons why the mass had not shown up until now. We did not realize it at the time, but Shereene had gone to the bathroom and thrown up. She was overwhelmed with all the technical conversation and the thought of removing her breast. It was just too much for her. Like I stated earlier, breast cancer is not only a physical assault; it is also emotional. We were deeply engrossed in our conversation when Shereene interjected, "Hey, you two, how about explaining what you are talking about to the *patient*?"

When I heard her, it forced me to come back and face what my sister was going through. I wanted to be strong by being a doctor for her, but I had been trying to block out the feelings and the emotions that accompany knowing that a sibling has cancer. But right now, she needed me to be her sister. With that, we both looked over and included Shereene in the conversation and the decision making. Was it not her breast and her decision that we were talking about? Sometimes as a doctor, I have to make decisions for my family and their health situations, and I have a tendency to cut right to the core with my style. I had to realize this was different—this was cancer. It was not a common cold or a decision to take medication or not. Rather, it involved one of the core aspects of who a woman is— her sexuality and what makes her different from a man.

The decision to remove a breast should not be taken lightly. Knowing that Shereene might be having difficulty making the right decision, I asked her surgeon, "What would you do if this were you?" She said, "I would have a mastectomy because I think in this situation it is the best course of treatment." That sealed Shereene's decision as well as mine.

Her surgery went well, and she had a total of four courses of postoperative chemotherapy. The treatments made her quite ill, so my mother stayed with her until she improved. Throughout that time, we talked often. She was extremely sick with nausea and vomiting from the chemotherapy. She experienced such fatigue that it was a challenge for her to walk out in her backyard to the pool. At times she would be so angry with Mom for forcing her to eat. She hated anything with a pink color because it reminded her of Adriamycin, one of the chemotherapy treatments.

I would try to give her words of encouragement, all the while struggling with why God would allow this to happen to my sister. I just did not understand. The struggle must have appeared on my face because one day after church our church secretary said to me, "My gosh, Taffy, your sister has cancer, but it's not a death sentence. So don't put her in the grave. Trust and believe in God." That made me snap out of it. I started praising the Lord that Shereene was alive—she was sick but alive.

Mom and Shereene's husband, Jerry, remained a great support, and she finally started to improve a few months after the chemotherapy was over. By Christmas, she was sounding like her old self again and ready for Mom to return home. She was grateful our mother had been there with her. Being a nursing assistant, Mom was able to discern when she saw that Shereene was in trouble because she was not eating properly or when she was suffering from dehydration. She was also aware of the emotional crisis that can accompany cancer treatments. Mom was not shy about calling the doctor to get help for Shereene when she needed it.

The Christmas after her last treatment, Shereene sent out a Christmas card with a picture of her entire family enclosed. She wore a hat, and it was obvious that she was bald. But to my surprise, everyone in the picture was smiling—even my brother-in-law, who is always grumpy! The message in the card read: *"Praise God that He has gotten me through one of the most difficult times of my life. If this is how I had to get to know Him, then I'm the better for it!"* After reading her words, I prayed, "Lord, I cannot believe that Shereene is saying this. Can I learn from her lesson *without* going through such a trial?"

Shereene visited Marie and me the following spring. When we saw her, we said the same thing, "You look better than both of us, and we didn't have cancer. Were you really as sick as you reported?" She answered, "Yes, and I praise God for getting me through the storm." Marie and I could not believe our eyes or ears. Throughout dinner, we couldn't help but stare at her. I don't even remember the meal as much as how great she looked. She had a short haircut, had gained weight, and was walking tall. Shereene had always had long, beautiful jet-black shoulder-length hair and was very trim in size. Her new weight looked very appealing on her; besides, Marie and I always thought she was too thin.

We knew a miracle had taken place in our sister! Not only had God healed Shereene, but she also had a closer walk with Him. She was praising God *for* her illness! We were astonished, and all the way home, I kept thinking to myself, *God, You are awesome.* I had just seen a miracle take place right before my very eyes. How could someone as sick as she had been still praise God and keep her sanity? I just didn't understand. Again, I uttered the prayer, "Lord, let me learn from my sister, but I *don't* want to learn it the way *she* had to do it."

In looking back, the one treasure I learned about God is: *We all have unique experiences that He designs specifically for each one of us.* We do not get to choose our troubles; God does. So even though I was praying not to experience a storm like my sister's, God was preparing one not only for me, but also for Marie.

Before her journey with breast cancer, Shereene reported she only had a casual relationship with Jesus. But because of her experience and closer walk with the Lord, she is a changed woman. Now as an active member in her church, she sings in the choir, helps with the youth, and serves on the usher board.

Shereene comforts other cancer patients and was a great consolation to her friend who died of ovarian cancer. She also shared in the spiritual journey with her sister-in-law who developed breast cancer. On her job, countless people have come to her office privately to speak to her about her walk with the Lord and to get advice about God. Some of them have even come to faith in the Lord Jesus Christ.

I even noticed a change in me. My sister's breast cancer made a strong impact on my life and caused me to make a huge difference in the way that I spoke with patients and their families. As a family member who has witnessed a close sibling overcome cancer, I found myself better able to connect and communicate with my patients, particularly those with cancer or some other catastrophic illness. I had more insight into what the diagnosis of cancer meant and could respond to the hopelessness and despair they were feeling. With cancer patients, I could truly empathize with them when I diagnosed their cancer. I remember one patient in particular who was diagnosed with uterine cancer. When I told her that she had cancer, she looked at me in disbelief and began sobbing with her face buried in her hands. I was able to give her some genuine hope, speaking with a sincere heart.

The newfound appreciation I had for the family members who were going to come alongside the loved one with cancer was more apparent to me. I was able to consider my patient's husband, include him in the care plan, and tell him what he was about to endure. I told him that he could make it through with God's help. It was all a reality for me now, and I had learned to speak about it from my heart. I would mention my sister and give them encouragement by telling them that, though the road was going to be rough, I had seen my sister survive by the grace of God. I could offer them hope too. Hope started to infuse my conversations with my cancer patients, because I had seen firsthand what God could do in a life that surrenders to Him in the midst of a storm.

Shereene continued to do well and her biannual checkups detected no recurrence of cancer. I continued to think about how she would do over the next years, but now with a different outlook. Knowing of her newfound faith and belief in the Lord Jesus Christ, somehow I could place her in His hands and be assured that He had already turned her situation into good and received His glory. Each year as she continued to do well, this new hope I had for Shereene transferred to my cancer patients. I continued to praise God for her healing with a wonderful testimony for my patients. I could also encourage them to press on and continue their treatments, even though it was tough.

Shereene wanted to help with the fight against breast cancer and became a volunteer with the American Cancer Society and helped encourage women with breast cancer. She also participated in some of the national breast cancer research trials. In one of the trials in which she was a participant, the researchers found that the experimental drug that she was on helped reduce the recurrence of breast cancer compared to the placebo (sugar pill). After a diagnosis of breast cancer, the pathology report will reveal if receptors for the hormones estrogen and progesterone are present in the tumor. If the hormone receptors are found, the doctor will put the patient on medication to suppress these hormones. In particular, estrogen can increase cancer growth and thereby cause a possible recurrence of cancer cells after the treatments are over. Therefore, suppressing estrogen with medication, such as the drug tamoxifen, has been proven to decrease the recurrence of breast cancer.

Because Shereene had positive estrogen and progesterone receptors in her tumor, she was placed on the drug tamoxifen to decrease the risk of recurring cancer. Tamoxifen has been studied extensively and has been shown to decrease the recurrence of breast cancer, but it has only been proven to be effective for five years after treatment. Researchers had no other drugs to continue combating the disease when patients were taken off tamoxifen and the risk of cancer could increase.

Shereene participated in the trial to determine if another class of drugs similar to tamoxifen would help reduce the risk of breast cancer recurrence after the first five years of taking tamoxifen. I remembered her calling me to say that her oncologist had asked her to participate in the study. She wanted to know what I thought about it. We discussed the great opportunity to help support the research in breast cancer that could benefit thousands of women. During the conversation, I could actually hear the excitement in her voice at the thought of helping other breast cancer patients.

As a result of this trial, the researchers were able to discover that this new class of drugs, called aromatase inhibitors, would help reduce the recurrence of breast cancer. They had found a drug that works beyond the five years of tamoxifen therapy to help reduce the recurrence of cancer for yet another five years. When Shereene's oncologist told her the good news that they had found a drug that was successful and that she was on that drug as a result of participating in the study, we were all surprised. Mostly we were grateful that God had led her to participate in a research trial to help others—and she had received the benefit as well.

After going through treatments for breast cancer, or any cancer for that matter, most women are understandably tired of taking medicine. This is especially true after completing a drug like tamoxifen, which has many side effects, including muscle and joint pain. There is also the risk of exposure to uterine cancer. The majority of people would reject taking further treatments, let alone undergoing an experimental study. But there are some women out there who want to do all they can in the fight against breast cancer and are willing to participate in research trials. As a result, these courageous women really do make a difference.

The study was a huge advancement because it not only enables doctors to decrease the risk of breast cancer using a new class of drugs, but most recently they have found that they can go directly to this class of drugs for some patients and skip tamoxifen altogether since these drugs work better at reducing cancer recurrence than tamoxifen. I thank God for Shereene and the many other women who agreed to participate in this and many other cancer studies. When she joined the study, I'm sure Shereene never knew what impact it would have on the lives of many women, including the future of her two sisters.

When I think of Shereene's experience with breast cancer and the woman she is now, I'm reminded of the Scripture in 2 Corinthians 1:4 where Paul wrote about God, the Father of all comfort, *"Who comforteth us in all our tribulation, that we may* be able to comfort them which are in any trouble, by the comfort wherewith we ourselves are comforted of God."

Treasure

Each one of us has unique experiences that God specifically designs for us. We do not get to choose our troubles; God does. And if we are smart, we will use these experiences to help someone else.

THE DENIAL:
AND HOW
I MET "A ROCK"

I had only been married two years when Shereene was diagnosed. My husband, Roland, was a great support to me during her illness. He saw how my family cared for one another, and he prayed faithfully for us as we supported Shereene.

Roland was all that I wanted in a marriage partner. I met him at a Chinese restaurant on a blind date that was arranged by one of the resident doctors at Pennsylvania Hospital. I was in a practice owned by that hospital, which is one of the most prestigious in the city. At that time, I was on top of the world. I had everything I needed for what I considered the "good life." I was a doctor who had good friends, a loving family, and I was making great money. I was surrounded by many single males and was ready to settle down.

One day I was watching *The Oprah Winfrey Show* when the announcement came on that they were going to do a future program on dating. The announcer invited people to send in a letter describing their idea of "the perfect mate." Often over dinner, my girlfriends and I would talk about what we wanted in a husband. We filled our journals and thought deeply about the issue of marriage. Since we were all Christians, the criteria at the top of the list was that the men we would marry must be Christians. Beyond this, we were looking for various characteristics, such as: men who were good at making money, hardworking men, good-looking men, tall men, men who liked to travel, and so on. I recall how one friend said that she would never marry a man who did not earn six figures. And to this day, she remains unmarried. When they asked me what I wanted in a husband, my response was, "All I want is that he knows the Lord." When I met Roland and shook his hand, I felt that he was different from the other men I had dated. By the end of the night, I *knew* he was different. He was a pastor, and all he talked about was how he loved the Lord and his journey with God. Roland had traveled the world and had studied in Israel. Most important, he was committed to God's calling on his life to be a pastor. He was fulfilling the call by pastoring at a small church outside of Philadelphia. *Wow,* I thought, *could this be for real? A good-looking man who has his eyes on the Lord and is serious about serving God!*

In my past relationships, I had proven that I was not a good judge of character, so I didn't trust my ability to choose the right mate. I had become completely frustrated with dating. Instead, I decided to stay home every night, reading my

Bible until God brought a husband to me. Through prayer, studying the Word of God, and practicing much discipline, I was willing to wait until God chose my mate. I prayed that He would remove any man from my life who was not to be my husband *before* I developed feelings for him. Consequently, the guys I met would never call me back. But my future husband was different; he kept calling back.

Several of us attended this blind date. I was to meet Roland, and a male friend of mine from residency was to meet a female resident doctor who worked with me at Pennsylvania Hospital. Of course, two of my best friends, Jean and Joni, were in attendance also. They knew what I was looking for because we shared our journals. When they saw Roland, they immediately liked him as well. He was drop-dead gorgeous! At the least, he was six feet seven inches tall, wearing a tailored suit and a nice watch, and he drove a Mercedes Benz (so much for our Christian journals).

My friend was so busy listening to Roland's and my conversation about Roland's extensive travel throughout the world that he could not enjoy his own date. He kept interrupting us and telling me that I was pronouncing Roland's name wrong. Roland had told me to call him Hayes, which is his middle name. But I could not get it right, and I kept calling him Hoss instead. I was so embarrassed; I wanted to tell my friend to butt out of our conversation. Then he finally got the hint from a mean glare that I gave him, and he left us alone—but only for a while. He was so jealous of Roland's Mercedes that he almost crashed his own car watching Roland drive off.

Roland was just so amazing; I could not believe my eyes.

Every time I would glance across the table at my girlfriends during dinner, they would give me the thumbs-up. We had a nice conversation about God, and by the end of the night, I knew that he really loved the Lord. I could hardly believe that a professed Christian man could be this dedicated to God, this cool, and, at the same time, be so nice!

Since Roland had been late for our date and had to leave early, I did not give him my number that evening. I thought that maybe he would go the way of the others, but soon after that night, he asked my resident friend to find out if he could call me. Of course, I said, "Yes!" When he called me one evening, he told me that he was looking for a mate—a future wife—and that he wanted to date me. I was shocked, but I asked God to guide me if this was truly the man for me. The Holy Spirit led me to the Scripture, *"Blessed is she who has believed that what the Lord has said to her will be accomplished!"* (Luke 1:45 NIV). I pondered over this verse for months and started thinking that this was the Lord's response to my asking Him for a mate. Roland fit everything in my journal—he was a Christian and he loved the Lord. It was that simple; I had not asked for much more than that. So, I believed that this was God's approval of the marriage, and I just needed to accept it.

For the next two and a half years, we dated off and on. Whenever I had doubts about whether Roland was the man for me, the Holy Spirit would bring to my remembrance this same Scripture. I prayed that God would give him to me only if this was the man for whom I was to be a helpmate. Moreover, my desire was that I would be able to hold Roland up in prayer as a wife should. Knowing how difficult marriage could be in any circumstances, I asked the Lord to allow me to marry Roland only if this was His will. It took the Holy Spirit to bring me to a place where I could pray a selfless prayer and exercise self-control over my life during this time of seeking God's wisdom and guidance. By relying on God, I had come to want only what was best for Roland. If I was to be the woman for him, then I was confident that God would bring us together.

In June of 1996, much to my surprise and that of my family, we eloped to Virginia. I had always wanted a big wedding, but Roland did not. We had started making plans for a small wedding, but it was turning out to be too big, and we called it off. Then my sister Marie said, "If you two are going to get married, you might as well elope." We thought about it and knew that we just wanted to be together. Since we could find no reason to be apart any longer, we took my sister's advice—and we did it.

After the excitement of our marriage and telling all my family, and especially my girlfriends, I settled in and knew that God had answered my prayer to become Roland's wife. So the package was now complete. I was a doctor, a wife, and the first lady of my husband's church. With my new husband I moved to the church's parsonage in Pottstown, which is about an hour outside of Philadelphia.

A few years before we were married, I believed that God was leading me to be more of a witness for Jesus Christ. I felt that the Lord was calling me to offer my medical services to the underserved population in Philadelphia. I sensed that He wanted me to work with an underserved population by giving them the best medical care possible. Therefore, I left the prestigious practice at Pennsylvania Hospital and went to work at

Misericordia, an inner-city Roman Catholic hospital that was committed to serving the underserved. This, I was certain, would fulfill the call that the Lord had placed on my life.

Before I left Pennsylvania Hospital, I had begun witnessing to patients about Jesus Christ. One of them complained to my associates, calling me a "religious zealot." Two of my associates asked me to stop speaking about Jesus and my faith, but this was not an option for me. Christ had such a hold on my life that I desired to live every aspect of it to His glory. My life was now His. Immediately after the conversation with my associates, I phoned one of my best friends who was also a Christian and an associate in the practice. I told her what they had said to me. Barb's response was, "I must not be doing a good job at witnessing because they didn't ask me to stop." We both laughed and agreed that we needed the Lord's guidance. So Barb and I prayed and waited for God to show us the next step in our careers. We knew that He had a plan. At the same time, our group of associates had decided to separate in one month. That would leave Barb and me on call in our own practice every other night. We were prepared to do this if this is what God was calling us to do.

One week before all this started to happen, I received a call from the gynecology chairman at Misericordia Hospital. He asked me if I was interested in ministering to their patients, both medically and spiritually. I declined at the time because I had just made a commitment to my associates and the hospital for another five years. I needed to honor my contract. I knew that Misericordia serviced an underserved area and thought that it would be ideal for me. Since I had prayed about this six months earlier, I even believed that God had called me to do this very type of service. But I also knew that I needed to honor my word—unless God saw fit to break the contract.

When I was asked by my associates not to share Jesus with the patients, I was very sad. I really liked my partners, and I loved working with the resident doctors in training. More important, I was fond of the patients and pleased with the fact that I could share Christ openly with them (or so I thought). When I discussed all this with Roland, he told me to wait on the Lord and reminded me that I could rely on God's faithful direction to see me through. He knew that I really had a heart for the Lord and wanted to incorporate Him into my practice. He pointed out that God would open a door for me to fulfill His will if He was calling me to do this.

During the week that all this was happening, I prayed constantly and felt much anguish about the thought of being on call every other night. Then the Lord reminded me of the phone call I had received a week earlier from the chairman at Misericordia. I thought to myself, *Yes, this must be it!* I called him and asked if they were still interested in me for the position as an OB/GYN. I even asked if they would consider Barb also. The chairman replied, "Yes." Barb and I were ecstatic!

After the interview with the chairman, we met with the chief financial officer and accepted the positions. Both Barb and I now had other jobs doing exactly what God had called us to do—all in one week's time. We could discuss our faith freely and openly while we practiced medicine. We praised God and rejoiced in Him. Roland was also happy, and I was thankful for his spiritual guidance throughout this dilemma. The treasure I learned is: *God is faithful, and when He closes one door, He will open another one that is part of His perfect plan.* And that He did. Not only were we able to witness to patients, we also got a raise. To top it all off, we were on call less often, which is the best gift that practicing obstetricians could receive. Yes, God is good.

I stayed at Misericordia for four years. It was great working with five other Christian doctors as we all shared our faith in Christ with the patients. It was truly a blessing. In fact, besides my new partners who were Christians, many of the staff members were Christians, including some senior management and some nurse midwives. And I was still working with my buddy Barb. She was one of the friends with whom I shared my journals when I was looking for a mate. We all had a good time at Misericordia, even though the work was hard and we put in long hours. I believe we made a difference in the community by showing people the light of Jesus Christ through the loving care and the medical attention that we provided for the patients. I firmly believe that this time of attending to the underserved community was when I found my true calling in medicine.

However, Pottstown, where Roland and I lived, is about fifty miles from the hospital. It was a long commute that left me extremely tired at the end of the day. Sometimes it was very hard to concentrate on the drive home in heavy traffic on the busy streets and highways of Philadelphia. Then a position opened up and I felt the need to transfer to St. Joseph's Hospital in Reading, Pennsylvania. This hospital was only twenty minutes from my house. Their OB/GYN clinic served an underserved community with a mostly Hispanic population. I was happy to be able to practice the Spanish that I had learned several years earlier when I lived in Spain with Shereene. At St. Joseph's I continued witnessing for Christ to my patients. I thoroughly enjoyed the staff and the patients at the clinic.

I worked hard and loved what I was doing, but eventually I realized that I was spending more time working *for* God than I was spending time *with* God. I had grown busier than I ever wanted to be, and my life was unbalanced. I shared my dilemma with Barb, who was married and living in New Jersey at the time. While I knew the work was important, I told her I didn't know how much longer I could keep up with the schedule. I felt emotionally and physically exhausted all the time. I was back to being on call every third night, delivering babies and working in a busy office practice. My husband heard my cries and informed me that God usually takes His children from one thing to another. He reminded me of how I had arrived at Misericordia and had then moved on to St. Joseph's. He was praying for me and told me to be faithful right where I was. When God uses Roland in his pastoral role to speak the truth to me like this, I sometimes forget that he is my husband.

I continued to pray for deliverance. This time it was not for Shereene; it was for me. All I wanted to do was slow down and spend time with my husband and family again. The pay was excellent, but I found that I had no time to enjoy it. More than anything, I wanted quiet time with the Lord. I wanted to know Him better, but I was usually too tired to read my Bible and pray. But when I did pray, I found myself praying Philippians 3:10, *"That I may know him, and the power of his resurrection, and the fellowship of his sufferings."* At times I would talk to

God and tell Him that I was not doing what the Scripture said, which was to get to know Him. How could I spend eternity with Someone I did not know? I loved reading my Bible and attending Bible study, but I was just too tired to do so. This did not look good for the first lady of the church. Moreover, I felt bad that I was missing the valuable teaching that I needed from my husband and pastor.

One year after taking the job at St. Joseph's Hospital, I knew that I had a breast mass. In fact, I had been praying for over a year for God to remove it. As I look back in my journal, it was there in October 1999. I had written that I thought it was a benign mass and had asked God to remove it. I really thought it was benign because it had a smooth and round appearance. I had not recorded the initial size in my journal, probably because I thought it was benign. I was certain that it was a fibroadenoma, a benign mass of the breast that grows large and usually slowly. I had pretty much convinced myself of this and thought I could get it taken care of sometime in the future if God did not perform a miracle. In March, 1988, I had had a breast biopsy that turned out to be fibrocystic changes that posed no risk. This was exactly what Shereene had had in her two benign breast biopsies before her cancer.

One year after my breast biopsy in March 1999, my primary doctor felt another mass, and I went back to my surgeon for an exam. It turned out to be only scar tissue. My primary doctor still believes that this was probably the mass that I was dealing with, and she might have been right. However, by the end of 2001, it had grown to the size of a golf ball, if not larger. Barb had seen me earlier in 2001, and I had even told her that it was

a fibroadenoma and not to worry. She told me to get a mammogram immediately to find out for certain and had even given
me a referral, but I didn't go.

Periodically I would see the slip on my desk, but I still did
not find the time to get the mammogram. Instead, I prayed
that God would remove the mass through my prayers of faith.
After all, I believed that I had the faith for Him to remove it. I
had even read many books on faith and healing that taught me
a great deal about having faith in God. Since I was doing God's
work, I reasoned, He would not want me to interrupt my busy
schedule; therefore, God would remove my mass. Nevertheless,
I kept this information from my husband. Since I had rather
large breasts, the mass could be concealed. I knew that he
would have scolded me even though I thought it was benign.
Roland would have told me to seek God in prayer but go and
get treatment, regardless of my busy schedule.

The treasure I learned here is: *God is faithful and He looks at
the heart.* Even though I delayed getting medical treatment, God
was having mercy on me until He brought me to the understanding that I needed treatment. In spite of all the excuses I had
given Him—especially the excuse of being too busy to take care
of myself while I was doing His work—God extended me grace.
I truly love God with all of my heart, and I truly thought that I
was indispensable because I had dedicated my work to Him.

This thinking is wrong; however, it is prevalent among
Christians and throughout the medical community as well.
Doctors can be the worst patients, because we have a tendency
to delay our own diagnoses and treatments. We put other people, our patients, before our own needs. And we're trained to

deny ourselves until we've taken care of everyone else. This is a daily occurrence as we carry out our duties; we skip lunch, dinner, and whatever else it takes to help the patients. We ignore our families and miss vital time with our spouses and children for the sake of our patients and the practice of medicine. It was never intended to be this way.

In the meantime, we do not realize how much we are hurting ourselves and our health in the long run. Rather, we should consider what good we can be to any patient when we are worn-out and cannot function any longer. In particular, what good are we when we let our own diseases go so far that we can no longer work because of the delay in getting diagnosed? Then, when we are unable to help patients anymore, much less ourselves, we are at the mercy of our very own colleagues.

In His own way, God was preparing me for the answer to my prayer to know Him. He was about to show me how to slow down and take care of my breast mass. He was preparing my own unique storm—one designed perfectly for me. Not only would He release me from the rat race in which I felt trapped; He would also provide circumstances that would lead me to a much deeper intimacy with Him than I had ever known.

I call my husband "a rock" because God gave him to me to be the voice of reason and stability in my life. I truly love my husband and thank God for giving me the perfect mate with whom I need to share this life. But I also know that Jesus is truly "the Rock," and Roland consistently points me to Him because He is the Sustainer of our lives—the One whom neither of us can live without.

Treasure

*God is able to use circumstances in your life, regardless of
how far you think you have come, and turn them into
something for your good and the good of others. This truth
is revealed to us in Romans 8:28, "And we know that all
things work together for good to them that love God, to
them who are the called according to his purpose." God is
merciful and looks at your heart. If you truly have a heart
for God and desire to know the truth about Him and His
ways, through His guiding hand He will show you His way.
It is never too late to follow God's will.*

3

THE DIAGNOSIS: "NO, NOT ME!"

As I sat on the side of my bed doing my devotions on a cold winter morning, I reminded God of the breast mass that He had not yet taken care of. It was January 22, 2002, and I was still praying that He would perform a miracle and remove it supernaturally. If any of my patients had waited to come and see me with a mass this size, I would have scolded her. But I was still too busy to get myself checked out—too busy to take time for myself. My focus was on doing the Lord's work. In addition to being a pastor's wife, I was a Christian doctor in a busy hospital-based practice—on call every third night, as well as teaching medical students and residents.

I thank God that being a pastor's wife did not entail much

responsibility at our church because I could not have handled it. My church family is so great. Knowing of my heavy responsibilities as a doctor and a wife, they really did not ask me to do much in the church. I am grateful to God that we have capable and dedicated deaconesses and pastor's aides who really do much of my job. Nevertheless, I still felt obligated to be present at all the functions the church was having; that is, until I suffered from such exhaustion that my husband intervened and prevented me from doing so any longer. Yet I continued to attend our women's monthly luncheons because I loved being around the ladies of my church and cherished the opportunities to hear their wisdom.

Although having time for my personal life beyond the practice of medicine was an issue for me, I devoted any leisure time that I did have to the joy of traveling with my family. At least once every three months, in spite of how busy I was, I would look forward to visiting the islands, such as the Bahamas or Puerto Rico, baking out in the hot sun on the beach and watching the waves endlessly going back and forth. But I was really convinced that I did not have enough time to take care of my personal needs, much less allow myself time off sick. I had read many books on healing. One book especially stuck out in my mind. It was written by an OB/GYN doctor who had witnessed a woman supernaturally healed from ovarian cancer. I laid my demanding schedule and this woman's experience before God as reminders of the miracle for which I had been praying.

Another treasure I learned in darkness is: *Do not dictate to God.* I am not so essential to God's eternal plans that His work would stop if I got sick. It was pride and arrogance to think so, and God related this secret to me through a patient He sent my way.

After finishing my devotions one day, I rushed off to work. My partner asked me to see a former nurse of his in order to rule out uterine cancer. He said that she was an extremely good friend of his, with whom he had a long-standing friendship from his prior practice. She had called him the night before and told him that she was having problems with her menstrual cycle. Knowing she was a survivor of three separate cancers, he told her to come in immediately the next day to see me. All the while he was giving me her history, I thought he probably had it incorrect, because it seemed impossible that someone could survive three separate cancers and still be alive.

Before I entered the examination room, the medical resident gave me the woman's history, and it confirmed what my partner had said. I could not believe it. When I walked into the room and greeted her, I immediately asked her, "Are you sure you have been treated for three separate cancers?" This stunning, petite woman sat on the exam table, opened her mouth with a wide and warm smile, and showed no obvious concerns of previous cancer on her face when she replied, "Yes." *This is impossible,* I thought, as we reviewed her history. However, after talking with her, it became quite apparent—her history was accurate.

"But how did you survive two separate battles with breast cancer and another battle with cancer of the chest wall?" I asked. She explained how she had developed a rare cancer of her chest wall and axilla (underarm) at a young age , which took doctors a long time to figure out. Once she was treated for that cancer, she developed breast cancer in one breast. The breast cancer was then treated; and a few years later, she developed cancer in the other breast. And they happened to be two different types of cancer. She could prove that because the pathology reports for each cancer of the breast confirmed that they were different. So it was not a recurrence in the other breast.

I was astonished; I stopped taking notes and put my pen down to listen to her story. She shared how she had struggled over the years, but she was still able to attend nursing school and enjoy life—with God's help. She firmly believed that He had spared her life for a reason. She went on to tell me that each time that a mass appeared, she did not allow her past history of cancer, her fears, or her busy schedule deter her from getting treatment. I immediately said to myself, *Oh, no, God, You are speaking to me here.* This lady looked like the picture of health as she sat there discussing the possibility of a fourth cancer.

Furthermore, she was not even fifty years old yet; she was only in her early forties! She just chuckled at my astonishment and restated how she believed that God had kept her alive for a reason. Having been through a lot, she felt that she was unquestionably a better person after going through her illnesses. I told her right then that she may have thought her visit was to find out about a fourth cancer; however, she was also there to help me come to the realization of something I needed to do.

As I conducted her exam, I tried not to think about what I believed God was telling me to do, which was to go and get treatment for my breast mass. I said good-bye to this patient and told her that I would be in touch. Strangely, I turned to the medical resident working with me that day and said, "I know there is something that I need to do for myself—and soon; because of this woman, I'm going to get it done." I told her, "Being too busy is not an excuse to not getting yourself the proper personal care." Later that day, I walked into a nurse's room in the clinic and told her that I had a benign breast mass and needed a good female surgeon. I asked her to recommend one. She gave me the name of her surgeon, whom she had used for a breast biopsy that turned out to be benign. I thanked her for the number and put it in my lab coat.

As I pondered my patient's words and story throughout the day, I said to the Lord, *If You can get her through three cancers and interrupt her schedule for three different operations, I know that You can get me through whatever it is that I have. It is probably benign, but now I know that I need to stop and take care of it.*

I continued to insist that the mass was benign because of its smooth appearance. Anything this big—I convinced myself—would have surely killed me by now if it were not benign. Even though the borders had started out smooth, they were becoming irregular around the sides of the tumor. Without considering my positive family history of breast cancer and the fact that Shereene had stage-two breast cancer just four years earlier—I just knew that God would not do *this* to me. I did not have the time to undergo cancer treatment. God knew this. I continued to pray for the miracle; but as I said, we *cannot* dictate to God.

That evening I experienced such an intense, throbbing pain in my breast. I thought about my patient's testimony again and knew that God had used her to speak to me. I promised myself that I would get a mammogram the following day. Although I still thought that the mass was a slow-growing fibroadenoma, I knew that I needed an ultrasound to determine if it was cystic or solid. Dictating my own medical care, I was doing what doctors have a tendency to do. I had overlooked the fact that Barb had told me before to get a mammogram immediately. I was putting the wrong spin on Jesus' statement, *"Physician, heal yourself"* (Luke 4:23 NIV).

The next morning, I went to our busy labor and delivery floor to perform one of the two cesarean sections scheduled for the day. Before the surgery began, I saw my friend, a gynecologist, in the doctors' call room. As I changed into my scrubs, I told her that I had a breast mass that was probably a fibroadenoma. I informed her of my plan to have a mammogram that day and would have the results sent to her. I also told her that it was probably benign, and I was finally getting around to taking care of it. She said, "Okay," and I hurried on to do the first cesarean section.

The surgery went well. The baby came out crying, and everyone was happy. After talking with the family and writing my orders for the patient, I ran down to the radiology suite and asked the technicians (who were friends of mine and had performed many procedures on my patients) if they could fit me in for a mammogram. The girls agreed and were very nice to schedule me in right then. After the mammogram, I asked them to do an ultrasound to find out what type of mass I had. My breasts had always been cystic and large, and there had been several fibrocystic changes over the years. As a result, I could be rather difficult to examine.

I expected some initial uncertainty, but as the technician performed the ultrasound, her expression identified that I was in trouble. She kept saying, "Dr. Anderson, I see no cystic areas, only solid." She looked very concerned and asked me, "Which doctor do you want me to have come in and take a look?" I said, "What?" She restated the same words more emphatically, "Which doctor do you want me to have come in and take a look?" I thought to myself, *Who do I want to come in here and give me an opinion on my own mammogram and ultrasound?* I knew all of the radiologists fairly well and respected their opinions, and now one of them was going to give me an opinion on myself!

Oh, no, no way; this can't be happening! I thought to myself. But I gave in and asked for Dr. Park because he was always straightforward with a record of excellence in his diagnoses of clinical cases. I uttered in a despondent tone, "Dr. Park." To my surprise, he immediately came into the room. After he viewed the ultrasound and mammogram films, he spoke four words to me that I will never forget: "Taffy, this is tumor." With a stern face he looked me straight in the eye and said, "Go and get treated now." He then abruptly turned around and left the room, and I was left lying on the ultrasound table—in a state of shock.

The treasure I learned in darkness is: *God's grace can see you through any situation if you call on Him.* A portion of the Scripture in 2 Corinthians 12:9 came true for me, "My grace is sufficient for thee." There is no other way to account for how I made it off the ultrasound table and back to the labor and delivery floor, except by the grace of God. As Dr. Park left the room, the technician asked me if I was all right, and I uttered some words like, "I don't know." For the first time, the room, the ultrasound table, and the radiology area that I knew all too well had suddenly become the coldest place on earth. I felt like I was in a morgue; it was so dark. The technician asked me again if I was all right and said, "I bet you wish that you hadn't waited so long, huh?" I thought to myself, *That is* not *the right thing to say to someone at this time in their life.* But I knew that she did not mean any harm.

I remember saying, "God, help me." I sat on the side of the ultrasound table to catch my breath and just shook my head in disbelief about what I had just heard. Then God—and only God—guided my feet to the floor. Slowly, I started to walk out of the radiology suite and passed by all the technicians who knew by now what was happening. I gazed up at them and put on a brave smile. They looked very disturbed but gave me a smile. I knew they all shared my concern. God's grace stepped in right on time and guided me toward the delivery room. That was the longest walk of my life. People spoke to me, but I hardly understood them. I was in a daze. I had just been given what I considered to be a death sentence. The mammogram was a stage five (mammogram stage and cancer stage are not the same thing), the worst stage, the highest stage indicating obvious cancer (we now call it category five, which is the same), and I was the one who had this large cancerous tumor. From a medical standpoint, I knew all too well that my prognosis was not good.

As I approached the labor and delivery floor, I was paged to come and start the next cesarean. I prayed again, "God, please get me through this." Just as I finished the prayer, my partner showed up to help me with the operation. He was usually late, but at this moment he showed up right on time—or should I say, on God's time. I thanked God and greeted the next expectant parents. As I started to scrub, I thought about my husband, who was out of town at the time. *How am I going to tell him?* Then I thought about my family, *How will I break the news to them?* I also thought about Shereene's cancer and what she had gone through. I knew that I was in for the same, if not worse, because I was in a more advanced stage than she had been. Knowing my current state of mind, I asked my partner to take charge.

Deliveries are usually such a cheerful occasion, whether they are vaginal or cesarean, and this one was no different. Everyone in the room was laughing and talking as we performed the surgery. I had made a habit of conversing with the parents during the surgery, but this time I could not speak a word. I focused myself on the task at hand and the need to keep my mind off the diagnosis I had just been given. I kept thanking God that Drew had shown up to take charge and had become the primary surgeon, leaving me as the assistant. However, with everyone talking and acting so jovially, I wanted to scream out, "Don't you all know I've just been given a death sentence? Stop this rejoicing!"

But by God's grace, I made it through the operation. I was experiencing a flood of emotions: from numbness and denial (*No, this is not really happening to me*); to horror (*My God, it really is me!*); and then shock and disbelief (*No, not me!*). After the baby was delivered, I felt a sadness begin to envelop me. I wanted to cry and scream at the same time.

Just before a tear ran down my cheek and into my surgeon's mask, a nurse called into the room and requested me to scrub out; I was needed for an emergency delivery. I was so grateful for the distraction because I felt the sadness was about to overwhelm me. I struggled with the emotions that were raging through my mind. One minute I was sad, the next, angry at myself for thinking the mass was benign, and finally I felt horrified at the thought of the treatment I would have to endure. But mostly I felt sadness. Not only did I have cancer; I would not be able to care for the patients whom I loved to serve. I would no longer have the privilege of working with the great staff at the hospital. Overall, I knew that I truly loved medicine and taking care of patients. These things gave me much joy in spite of how busy I was and how much I complained about being overworked. I truly loved delivering the babies and watching them bond with their mothers after they were born.

After getting my results, Dr. Park had called my friend, the gynecologist whom I had spoken with in the doctors' locker room. She told me to go home immediately and take care of the situation. She was so concerned that she had even asked my partner to cover for me. As I prepared to leave, I recalled that I had made an appointment with a breast surgeon for the following week. I phoned again and asked for an earlier date. Initially they said there were none available, but when I called back, there was an opening for the next day. I felt a sigh of relief and knew this was divine intervention—proof that God was continuing to watch over me.

I told my partner what was happening. He gave me a big hug and offered me words of reassurance, sharing that his mom is a breast cancer survivor for more than fifteen years and is still doing well. I was encouraged that someone had survived for so long. I also remembered Shereene, who was already four years out from breast cancer and doing well. Considering these good reports, I was somewhat encouraged. I went back to change my clothes in the doctors' call room, where my day had started with the exuberance and hope of bringing new lives into the world. Now, in the face of tremendous uncertainty, I headed for home.

As I walked off the labor and delivery floor, some comforting words came to me from the Lord. This was the deliverance for which I had been praying. It was through this experience that God was going to answer my prayer for greater intimacy with Him. I remembered the Scripture on which I meditated: *"That I may know him, and the power of his resurrection, and the fellowship of his sufferings"* (Philippians 3:10). I just kept repeating in my mind, *I will know Him; I will know Him. Taffy, through this experience, you will know Him.*

But as I left the hospital that day, I somehow knew that I would never return to that kind of practice of medicine again. Since I had graduated from residency, there had been this fast-paced schedule of seeing so many patients throughout the day. When I was covering the hospital, I was constantly running back and forth—making rounds by visiting patients in their hospital rooms, delivering babies, performing surgeries, teaching medical residents and students, and covering the emergency room—all in one day. Not to mention the days I would be in the office, seeing the numerous patients scheduled; I could hardly talk to them for any extended period of time because of the demand to see so many patients in a day. Lastly, I was on call every third night. Even though a nurse midwife was doing most of the deliveries at night, I would often be called to come in to perform a cesarean section or any other surgery that was needed. Such extremely demanding duties would not be good now—for the patients or me. I had such a keen sense that this hurried lifestyle of mine was about to change dramatically. Moreover, I had asked for the change specifically because I wanted more time with God—so that I could better know Him.

In fact, I had never thought that such intense activity resulted in the best care for patients. I reflected on the several years since I had graduated from medical school and how hard I had worked. The time that I had spent with my patients dealing with the details of their diseases ran through my mind. In doing the Lord's work, I had even had the opportunity to share Christ with many patients over the years. In fact, I had taken care of scores of patients, passionately serving them and doing a good job, at that—but I had not taken care of myself. And now, what use would I be to the Lord? I concluded that this busy lifestyle was to my detriment. Nevertheless, at that moment, a strange peace comforted my troubled mind. Again, I knew this was God's way of removing me from the roller coaster I'd been on. Although I did not like the way He chose to answer my prayer, I felt I was going to be okay.

However, by the time I got home, I was a basket case all over again. I sobbed with disbelief, forgetting what God had just told me. My mind focused on the stage-five mammogram results that I had received and the medical implications of such a diagnosis. Why had I waited so long? Why did I allow myself to get so busy? Was this a form of denial? How could I have thought this huge mass was benign, knowing my positive family history? How could I have ignored my own health? I went on and on. I thought to myself, *I'm going to be an embarrassment to the medical community! Some doctor I was. The whole hospital will be laughing at me. All the degrees and outstanding teacher awards are not going to help me now!*

I knew that the treatment would be extremely difficult to go through, and I was sure God had chosen the wrong person. How could I ever endure this kind of suffering? Then God's peace came upon me again. It was such a sense of peace that I could not describe it. I knew that He was there with me. Although I was alone in the house, I knew I was not really alone. Because of my baffled state of mind, I could not think of any Scriptures at the time; I am sure that is why God's peace enveloped me.

When someone gets diagnosed with cancer or any serious illness, it is not unusual, and is probably the norm to experience a flood of emotions. I have witnessed some people become deathly silent, while others become panic-stricken in disbelief. Whatever the emotional response, believe me, there is going to be one. That's why, when there is a possibility that a doctor has to deliver life-threatening news, it is generally best for someone to be with the person to provide support. In particular, doctors are very careful during the first encounter in giving the diagnosis of a life-threatening illness to a patient. We know to expect the unexpected in patients' responses; therefore, we try to comfort them in the best way possible, for whatever emotions they might display.

People take bad news in many different ways, and the initial encounter is always the most difficult and shocking. In fact, horror and disbelief are just a couple of the feelings that may be experienced. One minute, the person may appear to be okay and have it together, and the next minute that individual may fall apart. On the other hand, someone else may have it all together and be able to handle the news with a completely positive outlook. As a physician, I have seen the whole gamut of emotions in patients. And regardless of what I had observed and who I am—that is, a doctor and a Christian who loves the Lord and knows His Word—I too had an intense emotional reaction at the time of my diagnosis. Working in the medical field and being a Christian did not make me immune to the intense pain and fear that comes with the diagnosis of cancer.

By the grace of God, I pulled myself together enough to phone my husband, who was in Myrtle Beach attending a ministers' conference. I called him and said, "You need to come home right now. I have just been given a diagnosis of cancer." At first he was silent for what seemed to be a lifetime, and then he finally said, "What? Are you sure?" I responded, "Yes." His voice cracked when he said, "I'm on my way home."

Before I left for the airport to pick up Roland, I phoned my sisters and my mom. I remember Marie was driving, but I could not hold back from telling her. She could hear something was wrong in my voice. I said, "I have breast cancer." She had to pull to the side of the road, because after I told her, she started sobbing hard in disbelief. Her teenage daughter Jade was riding with her and said, "Mom, Auntie is going to be okay. Now get yourself together; we are going to go through this with her." Marie said that she just looked at Jade, the one who is usually sobbing and upset about everything; she was being surprisingly strong in the midst of this turmoil. She was glad Jade was with her.

That evening, as I drove to the airport, I kept thinking about how stupid I was by delaying getting the mass checked out. I thought back to a year ago when I had seen Barb and she had told me to get a mammogram. I certainly could not blame it on my best friend. When I called her, Barb just started crying and asked if she had misdiagnosed me. I told her that she had not. I just never did what she told me to do, which was to get the mammogram and stop diagnosing myself.

When I met Roland, he gave me the biggest hug ever. After we got in the car, we both cried. He suggested that it was probably better that he drive, and since I was emotionally exhausted from grief, I agreed. I handed him the keys and moved to the passenger's side. There was silence for a while in the car, and I started thinking, *Why is he not asking me how long it been there? Why didn't I tell him? How did this happen?* Instead of these questions, the unexpected occurred. As we rode along, he started talking about God's faithfulness. He reminded me that God is faithful and He would see us through this together. He remained a rock of assurance, as I still know him to be today—always positive in the midst of the storm—with his eyes centered on Jesus. God allowed him to see the higher good in this difficult situation, and Roland never scolded me or made me feel guilty.

Roland has never been much for words whenever we have been confronted by a trial. Rather, he would show his support by giving me God's Word and serving as a "Rock of Gibraltar" when we were faced with difficulties. This time would be no different. He remained a man of few words, but the words he spoke brought peace to my heart that night. Even though Roland does not talk a lot when faced with adversity, I can always tell from his facial expression that he is talking to the Father with the deepest concern for the situation. That night, it all showed on his face as he tried to hold back the tears and speak. He remained hopeful as he spoke of God's truth concerning healing—how Jesus had healed many people in the Bible—and that was where my healing was going to come from. Roland had always said, and reiterated it then, "As long as you are living, God is able to perform a miracle right up until your last breath, no matter how bleak the situation may appear to be."

As a medical doctor, I knew that my situation was bleak. However, he was speaking words of truth to my spirit about who God is and what God is able to do. By God's grace, that evening we were able to tell the rest of our family and friends. They, in turn, offered us words of support through their tears and disbelief. I continued to sob off and on with Roland holding me, and I know that he was praying for me. I'm not sure exactly what he was praying, but knowing my husband, he was probably asking God to comfort me, to guide us both, and to give us the grace to endure this storm. By the end of the night, Roland and I were sure of who God is—God is *faithful*. Equipped with this knowledge, we were ready to see the surgeon the following morning. So we held each other and drifted off to sleep.

Treasure

God is faithful in a storm. If you call on Him and acknowledge that only He can comfort you and see you through, by His grace He will guide you. His grace is sufficient for you and me.

4

THE BIOPSY AND TREATMENT PLAN: "OKAY, MAYBE ME"

The following morning we headed off to see a breast surgeon who came highly recommended by a nurse in my office. When we awoke, we were both pretty somber and spoke only a few words. My husband prayed with me before we left the house, and God's peace started to surround me like the wings of a dove—and a beautiful one, at that. I truly felt God's presence and His peace. I was glad that my husband had come home to be with me.

I wanted privacy, so I went to another hospital in town. The doctor had a very strong reputation for being a good surgeon with an excellent bedside manner. Being a female surgeon myself and observing other female surgeons, I came to believe that women surgeons are very meticulous. So, for comfort's sake, I wanted a woman surgeon. God answered that prayer and gave me a doctor in whom I could have confidence. I really felt that I could trust her.

While sitting in the exam room and waiting for the surgeon to come in, I started to realize how vulnerable we are when we're sick. In just twenty-four hours I had quickly gone from being a doctor caring for patients and giving orders to becoming a patient myself. Oh, at that moment I felt so helpless and scared. I thought to myself, *So this is what my patients go through.* Before the surgeon examined me, I warned her that what she was about to see would not be too pretty. When she separated my gown and saw the mass, her face never flinched, and, remarkably, she did not scold me. The only thing she said was, "Too busy to take care of yourself, huh? Well, now it is time to let me take care of you. Let's get down to business here."

She did a true-cut biopsy in the office and immediately sent it to the pathology lab. A true-cut biopsy involves the use of a special needle to take a portion of the abnormal tissue. When it is directed through the cancerous tissue, this instrument can retrieve a good tissue sample. The procedure can be performed in the office and sent to pathology for a quick evaluation. During the biopsy, my husband took my hand to comfort me while she passed the needle through the tumor. I felt like a two-year-old holding on to her daddy's hand. I have performed several office biopsies on patients, and I kept saying to myself, *So this is what it is like to have a biopsy.* And I didn't like it. The doctor then told me that she too thought this was cancer and that I would need chemotherapy prior to surgery. She ordered my blood work and X-rays and referred me to an oncologist.

I had promised the Lord that I would not attempt to treat myself or interfere with my medical treatment. I had already proven that I was not the best woman for the job. I promised to see whomever my surgeon recommended and to follow whatever treatment she decided to prescribe. With a cancer diagnosis, I knew the importance in following the recommendations of the primary doctor, who usually establishes working relationships and works hand in hand with other doctors. This enables the primary doctor to have confidence in the ability of those doctors to take care of their patients. Within only a few hours, I had broken this promise.

Later that evening, I contacted the same friend who helped us when Shereene was diagnosed with breast cancer four years earlier. She was now a leading researcher in breast cancer at the National Institutes of Health in Washington, D.C. She had given me invaluable advice when Shereene was treated for breast cancer. Now my friend was giving me good medical information; she even made recommendations for my treatment. But I soon realized that I had made a mistake in going back on my promise, when she told me that her team wanted me to come down to the National Institute of Health for a new experimental trial that was being conducted for large tumors.

When a person is diagnosed with cancer, the individual can elect to take the traditional medicine that most doctors offer for treatment. However, sometimes there is research going on that involves a particular stage and makeup of a tumor. In this case, experimental treatment may be offered that is proven to work but may be given at different intervals or dosages. She wanted me to participate in a research trial that would give me a chemotherapy regimen that was opposite the normal protocol. That meant I would start with Taxotere instead of the traditional Cytoxan and Adriamycin.

I ended up totally confused. Besides, I didn't like the fact that someone else was calling this a "large tumor." Where had she gotten that from? It was true, but I didn't want to hear the truth. Still, I had to face the reality of it all. I had given her the approval to speak with my doctor, and this it what she had been told. I kept thinking to myself, *So this is what it is like to be diagnosed with a serious illness.* I dreaded hearing the hard facts of my disease. Yes, at that moment I realized how hard it was to swallow the truth.

With the doctor asking me to come to Washington to be treated in the study protocol for large tumors, I had no idea what I should do. I confided in my husband, who remained a rock. He told me that it didn't matter where I went, that God could and would work through anyone, and I probably did not need to travel as far away as Washington, D.C. He kept pointing me to the Savior and reminding me to seek Him and to have confidence in God, not in the doctors.

Another secret I learned in darkness is: **When you're confused, be still before God.** While being still, you need to totally acknowledge who God is—that He is the almighty God. Then by knowing who God is, you are free to trust Him. This will allow you to keep from leaning on your own understanding of the situation. In my case, I knew all these people in medicine and could have gone to the most prestigious places to get treatment.

But I was getting confused about what I understood to be the best course of action for me. The answer to my confusion was to acknowledge God and His omniscience—His almighty power to know everything—including what was best for me in this situation. Ah, and lastly, if you do all of the above, He will then direct your path.

I did not know it at the time and could not fully express it, but what I was doing is stated in Proverbs 3:5–6: *"Trust in the Lord with all thine heart; and lean not unto thine own understanding. In all thy ways acknowledge him, and he shall direct thy paths."* To paraphrase Dr. Tony Evans of Oak Cliff Bible Fellowship, who explains the passage: Recognize that you know and completely trust God. Don't try to understand the situation with your own reasoning; rather, acknowledge that only God has the answer, and He will step in and show you what to do.

Taking this excellent advice, I became still before the Lord and prayed for discernment and guidance. Then God showed me that I should to stay at the community hospital and go through the treatment that was originally recommended by my primary surgeon. I didn't need to be concerned about a clinical trial or being treated at a prestigious institution. While I did not know all that was to come from this course of action at the time, I knew that God was orchestrating and fine-tuning what I was supposed to do. So I obeyed my husband and the voice inside my spirit. I told my friend that I was grateful for all of her advice, but I would be staying home for my treatment.

My surgeon told me that she would have the pathology report on the following Tuesday and I should call her then. It was Friday, which meant that I had to wait over the weekend

—but God was with me. He comforted me with such a sense of intimacy and reassurance at times during that weekend that I almost forgot I had cancer. That Saturday, I ventured out, and when I returned, I saw my husband sitting in the middle of the driveway with our dog, Ramsey. He looked as though he was in deep thought. He never told me what he was thinking, but I could tell that he was wrestling with God about something, which was probably my situation.

As his wife, I knew that when he was talking to the Lord about something, he would become very quiet until he had the situation settled before God and had received the answer. At this time, he was behaving the same way. As he and Ramsey moved aside, I drove up and asked, "Are you all right?" And he said, "Yeah." He was still in deep thought, I could tell. Later that week I knew that he was continuing to wrestle with God, until he came in late in the evening. He said, "I've been walking in the woods and talking with the Lord. God has given me a peace about this thing and has promised me your healing will take place through Him." He further stated, "God has promised me that He will see you through this, and I'm going to rest on His promises." Roland also said that he promised God that if He healed me, he would no longer sweat the small or the big things in life. He would hand them all over to God from here on out.

That day I saw a different man who remained firm in the Lord throughout my illness; he was the rock of stability that I needed so much. He constantly pointed me to God in times of my deepest discouragement and despair. Roland still says to this day that God was faithful to the promise He made to Roland about my healing.

Every husband, boyfriend, or significant other has different responses to their loved ones' diagnoses of breast cancer. As a physician, I have seen many responses from my patients' husbands to their illnesses. Some are in shock and cannot get over it, and some are in denial and act as if nothing is happening. They expect their women to carry on their duties as usual. Some have difficulty talking about such an emotional crisis and totally shut down. Some even leave their spouses. There are others who shower their mates with the emotional support that is needed. However, whatever the response, you must respect it and continue to go on.

The best thing to do is to try and open up the avenues of communication because women with cancer need to discuss their feelings and emotions. With Roland, my having breast cancer was an extremely emotional experience for him. There were times when I did not discuss it openly because of the pain I would see on his face. He handled my breast cancer by supporting me with his physical presence and the quiet assurance that he was there to care for my emotional needs. He spoke very few words about my condition and his own personal feelings, but he allowed me to openly talk about my concerns. Even today, I can still see the anguish on his face when we discuss my cancer. He really has difficulty sharing about it without shedding some tears.

On Sunday, my husband delivered the unexpected news to our church family. We have the most loving and supportive church family that any pastor and first lady could imagine. We truly are united as a family. When one person has pain or distress, we all feel it and pray for one another. Each branch of our auxiliaries consists of praying men and women. The deacons are my husband's backbone and are very supportive of him. He could not have wished for more spirit-filled men to undergird him. The deaconesses, pastor's aides, missionaries, choirs, and the entire Sunday school department are all welcomed support for us. The trustees have been so kind over the years; we could never repay them for their heartfelt benevolence.

So, when my church family heard the news, they were overwhelmed with sadness and confusion. Many of our members cried in disbelief. After the announcement, my husband turned around and openly wept in his pulpit chair. I felt so bad. All I wanted was the ability to take away their sadness, but there was nothing that I could do. I had already shared the diagnosis with my family. And my nieces Carla and Dionna, both of whom I'm very close to, who attended college and lived in the area, came and joined us for the service that morning. They had begun to cry even before my husband told the congregation. I remember that Dionna, who is very emotional, cried throughout the entire service. Feeling helpless, I just held her in my arms. Even my other niece Vicki and my nephew Herbert G, who were only twelve and eleven at the time, were very upset. In addition to my sisters Marie and Shereene, my four brothers—James, Jay, Saunders, and Harvey—were devastated. Harvey sent me the most wonderful card to encourage me.

After the service, there was a stream of people who offered me words of encouragement even through their tears. In fact, throughout my illness, my church family showered me with a wealth of love and prayers that I will never forget. Cards, flowers, and gifts poured into my home; the love and concern that I received was overwhelming. In addition to my church family, other people who knew me would also offer gifts and comforting words. My husband's friends and other pastors who were his fathers in the ministry blessed us with an abundance of phone calls that demonstrated their care and concern throughout my illness.

Some pastors would call me periodically and pray with me, such as Rev. James Edlow, senior pastor of Zion Baptist Church and Rev. Paul Cofer, associate pastor of Faith Fellowship Baptist Church. Others kept my husband busy by inviting him to preach at their churches. They would tell him how the whole church had been praying for me, and he would give them updates on my progress. All the local churches and even some of the local Christian organizations in Pottstown, where our church is located, were praying for us. When people called the church concerned about me and asked what they could do, Sister Shawell, our church secretary, said she told them to pray.

In particular, Rev. J. A. Jones would call me often; his church, First Nazarene Baptist of Camden, New Jersey, also kept me in constant prayer. Rev. Herbert Lusk, pastor of Greater Exodus Baptist Church, and his church members were holding my name before the Father, as well as the late Dr. William Augustus Jones, former pastor of Bethany Baptist Church, in Brooklyn, New York. These are just a few; I could not mention them all. However, I am indebted to them all, for I truly felt their prayers. Dr. Jones and Rev. Jones would take my husband to conferences during my illness to renew him and nourish him with the love and support that he needed. I also knew that my husband's father in the ministry, Dr. William L. Banks, pastor of Faith

Fellowship Baptist Church (my former church), his wife, and the church members lifted my name before the Father daily. They believed that God would heal me—whichever way God saw fit. He would turn this out for my good.

Another treasure I learned in the darkness is: *Carefully consider what you say in response to hearing that someone has entered a period of darkness, such as being diagnosed with a disease.* Never say: "It is going to be all right." Or "I know that God will cure you, He did it for me." People think that these are words of comfort, but they really are not, because no one is certain of what God will do. We cannot be sure if God will cure a person. But I knew that the people who said this had hearts that were kind and shared in my concerns. They just wanted to comfort me in some way, and the words they spoke represented their good intentions.

When people are sick, the body of Christ, (those who believe and follow the authority of the Word of God), should speak words of encouragement, but we *must* speak the truth. We must remind them that sometimes God showers His blessings upon us by removing our suffering. And other times God bestows His blessings by being with us through our suffering. As a result, I will say to people that I will pray for them and for their healing. I will ask God to give them the strength to bear whatever He decides to place in their lives. We need to focus our encouragement on what God has made known to us, like the fact that He is a good God and that nothing happens to us that is beyond His control. We should emphasize that God will ultimately use our trials for His glory and for our good.

I have learned to be silent about what God, in His perfect

knowledge and wisdom, has chosen at present to keep hidden from me. This is because I do not fully know what God is doing in my life. Therefore, I know even less about what God is doing in the life of another person. There are some people who have the spirit of discernment, who can perceive more clearly what God is doing in people's lives, things that the majority of us are unable to see. But even divine discernment does not provide the ability to predict what God will do in the future. This may seem to be a less reassuring way of comforting a person who is going through difficult times, but this is the way of truth—it is what the Bible teaches. We must honor God for who He really is, not for what we wish that He would be.

On a wintry but beautiful, sunny Tuesday afternoon, I called my doctor from my study to find out the results of the pathology report. She confirmed that, based on the report, I did, in fact, have breast cancer. It was an aggressive form of cancer, and she wanted me to start my treatments immediately. My husband was waiting upstairs but did not know that I had called. When I hung up the phone, I just sat in my chair for a moment; and what I had already known suddenly became a stark reality. It was as though it were written in stone. I went upstairs to our bedroom and told Roland, and we both cried once again.

Sister Shawell, our church secretary, and Brother Shawell are like our second parents. She called to see if we had heard anything, and we told her the news. Right on time, she started in with the most kind and supportive words that we both needed to hear about the Savior. She reminded us that He was not finished with me yet and that God was faithful and would see us through this. She exhorted us to keep our faith and eyes focused on Him. This precious sister knew what she was talking about since she had many close relatives in her family who have dealt with cancer. My husband responded to her, "I know you're right." He immediately started to see the good in the situation. After we hung up, he said, "Even though it looks bleak, Taffy, God is able to heal your cancer. And even if He does not, people can live with cancer for a number of years."

Roland called his parents and told them the definitive news. My mother-in-law, who I call "Grandma," reminded my husband of her cousin who had cancer and was living twenty years later. Her brother who had cancer was still living eight years after his diagnosis. Her own mother, who had cancer, lived another eight years after the doctors told her she would not survive two months. With these strong words of encouragement, I was able to face the next hurdle—the treatments.

I heard the stern plea in my surgeon's voice over the phone when she told me that I needed to start treatments immediately. It was time to put everything aside and take care of my own health. I promised her that I would. My bone scan, X-ray, and blood work all detected that the cancer had not spread. I could feel two lymph nodes in my armpit, and I was so grateful that the cancer had not spread past my lymph nodes. Cancer that has spread beyond the lymph nodes in the underarm indicates that it is at a more advanced stage and may be found in other areas of the body, such as the liver, bone, or brain. In this case, it is more difficult to treat. Although treatment is still possible, and many people are cured from this advanced stage, the level of treatments becomes more intense.

Even in the midst of this bad news, it became clear to me

that God was working. I had never seen anyone at my stage of cancer, with as large a mass as I had, who did not also have the disease spread beyond the lymph nodes into those other organs. When this occurs, it is called metastatic disease. I thanked God for controlling the disease in spite of my reluctance to get treated. He showed mercy on me by controlling my disease. God also gave me a Scripture on which to meditate, *"This sickness is not unto death, but for the glory of God, that the Son of God might be glorified thereby"* (John 11:4). Through this verse, God revealed to me that my sickness would contribute to His glory and would not result in my death. Only by the mercies of God could this be true, considering the time that I delayed in getting treatment. Essentially, this is what my husband had said to me after his walk in the woods and his talk with God that day.

Another treasure I repeatedly learned in darkness is: *You cannot box God into a corner and dictate to Him what you want Him to do.* I tried to tell God that I wanted a supernatural healing, and He did not comply. I had given Him all the reasons why He should heal me supernaturally—because of my busy schedule doing His work. I had dedicated my life to Him through serving those in need—but still He would not comply. So I had to go the natural way and seek treatment. It was then and only then, when I submitted to the Father's will, that I saw doors opening throughout my course of treatment. I was certain that His comforting hand was with me. You simply cannot dictate to God what He should do for you and think that He is going to do anything outside of His will. His will for me was to seek medical treatment in the natural way; He would heal me through that means, if He so decided.

Faced with advanced stage-two breast cancer—you could really call me a stage three that had not spread beyond my lymph nodes—I knew that I needed preoperative chemotherapy and a mastectomy. But I wanted no part of this. I would vacillate back and forth—one day, or even one minute, I would be okay, knowing that I could do this with God's help. Then, the next moment, I didn't want to face the inevitable. In despair, poor Roland watched my ever-changing moods. Believe it or not, I was still praying for a miracle that would allow me to avoid chemotherapy. But I deliberated with God and proposed that, if I went through chemotherapy, He would shrink it enough so that I would not need a mastectomy!

Well, again I was learning that I could not dictate to God how to run my life. Some people are healed by supernatural means, but I was not going to be one of those people. As I realized this, the more I experienced peace and restfulness. Rather than demand to be healed in the manner we choose, we must wait for God's answer. If you do not experience healing but continue to get worse, it means that God has a different plan for your life. Please learn from me. *Do not wait*; go and get treatment! Whatever treatment God prescribes, be assured that He is healing you through it. The Lord Jesus healed in many different ways—through spittle, a touch, or speaking a word, to name some of them. Remember that God, in Christ, is our healer.

Do not be deceived into thinking that it is the medicine that brings healing and fail to realize that God works through the medicine. My husband reminded me of this every time I would go for treatment. That way, I would not forget to give

God the glory instead of the chemotherapy, or whatever treatment I was getting at the time. Psalm 103:2–3 states, *"Bless the Lord, O my soul, and forget not all his benefits: who forgiveth all thine iniquities; who healeth all thy diseases."* It is God who heals all your diseases. How He chooses to heal is His business—not ours. Our business is to accept whatever method He chooses.

This truth was revolutionary to me because I had always separated God from science and healing. I believed that the medicine brought healing in a natural way, and that God only healed in supernatural ways. As a result, I was taught in medical school to leave God out of the healing process. We are taught that the medicine given to patients will assist in their healing, but ultimately the healing comes from the body's immune system. In the case of bacteria, the antibiotic kills the bacteria, but the body has to heal from the damage the bacteria causes. That is why you see a great deal of advancements in the research of drugs that enhance the immune response, because we know that the immune system plays such an important part in the healing process. However, God was never in the equation. But it is God who watches over the immune system, does He not?

Even when I rededicated my life to the Lord and began to learn more about Him, I would pray for my patients. But I still thought that I was responsible for healing them through the medicine I prescribed; therefore, I would take the credit. I never knew to give God the glory. As I went through my treatments, I started to realize that healing did not come through the doctors or the medicine. I developed a keen sense that God was healing me through the medicine and was perfectly orchestrating my healing, at that.

My husband would kindly but repeatedly remind me that healing was of God, and it was His decision to heal as He saw fit. Roland's proof was in making the observation of how two people having the same diagnosis and stage of cancer could take the same drug that has been proven to cure the disease, but one is healed and the other is not. He said that is because you cannot take God out of the healing process. Prayer, faith, and God's will combined determine if God will heal you through the medicine. God is our healer; He proclaims, *"I am the* LORD, *who heals you"* (Exodus 15:26 NIV). So, since God is the same yesterday, today, and forever, He is still in charge of healing and has not given it over to us physicians. Therefore, what I was learning about medicine and healing was in sharp contrast from what I had been taught in medical school. This would change my entire thinking about God and medicine.

The treasure I found through this illness taught me about God's healing. I learned that: *All healing comes from God.* He heals through medicine, which is the natural means; and He heals supernaturally, by not using medicine at all. To my surprise, my husband already understood this methodology and had not paid one dime to go to medical school!

Treasure

I learned many treasures in this part of the journey of my illness, but the one that became so clear to me is that all healing comes from God. And you cannot dictate to God how you want to be healed. God can heal supernaturally in the privacy of your home or wherever He chooses to do so. Or, if God chooses to heal through medicine given to you by your doctor, know that it is God in either case. According to Psalm 103:3, it is God who heals all of our diseases—and only God deserves the glory!

5

CHEMOTHERAPY: "THE PERFECT STORM"

When I met Dr. Lusch, I knew that I was in the right place for my treatments. He was such a soft-spoken man, with a warm and friendly smile, who also showed much emotional concern for me. This is unusual for a doctor. But as a colleague, I could sense that he knew what I was about to endure. He spoke with me, my husband, and my mom privately in his office. We discussed the treatment plan, and he said we should start immediately. The plan involved four courses of preoperative chemotherapy to shrink the tumor, a left mastectomy, two courses of postoperative chemotherapy, and radiation for six weeks. I was facing at least eight months of treatments, if all went well with my therapy. I agreed verbally, but in my heart I wanted no part of this treatment plan, especially the chemotherapy. As a resident physician, I had treated too many women with ovarian cancer over the years with the same chemotherapy he was about to give me—and I did not want it.

Chemotherapy is the usage of cytotoxic drugs to treat cancer. When I was in training, the cancer patients would be admitted to the hospital before their chemotherapy for IV fluids to prevent dehydration, since severe dehydration would occur with their treatments. I remembered being called as a resident to come and assess my patients because of their persistent nausea and vomiting. We would try all sorts of antinausea drugs, but to no avail. The chemotherapy treatment was so harsh on their systems; they could hardly walk from the fatigue and the numbness in their extremities. I remembered the hair loss and the pale and dusky skin color, especially in the younger women; many of them wore turbans on their heads. Seeing such frail bodies, I always felt so sorry for them.

There was one young lady in particular who was dying from choriocarcinoma, a rare cancer that can occur after pregnancy as a result of the placenta (afterbirth) becoming cancerous. She was so young, in her thirties, and we tried all types of chemotherapy to save her life. But she would become deathly ill from dehydration and a decrease in her white blood cell count, which made her susceptible to infections. Eventually, she surrendered to the disease, and I remember her mother being so devastated. Sadly, this woman left behind a very young child in her mother's care. So, yes, with such memories of treating women who had ovarian and other cancers that used this same and similar chemotherapies, I had firsthand knowledge about what it was going to be like. And I clearly wanted no part of this at all.

Mistakenly, I thought that I would still be able to be on call every third night while having my treatments. But after my first treatment, Roland and Mom took me to the emergency room with fever and chills due to strep throat, along with persistent nausea and vomiting from the chemotherapy. I was so scared from my reaction to the chemotherapy that I thought I was going to die. Subsequently, I called the hospital and took a medical leave of absence.

To my dismay, my hair soon started to fall out, and the rest of it felt heavy. This made me very sad. I had heard stories of how some people had not lost their hair, and I prayed that I would not lose mine. I knew there were various remedies that I could try, but I wanted to rely on prayer, and hope that God would preserve my hair—but He did not. About a week after my first treatment, I grabbed some of my hair that had fallen out and showed my husband, who warmly smiled and said it would come back. Roland was always a rock of encouragement for me. God had placed him in front of me to remind me of how things would get better. He calmly sat me down in the chair, took some scissors, and cut my hair.

The next day, more of it came out. The disappointment and anguish readily showed on my face. And this time, with such an adoring look, he took his shaver and shaved my head. To this day, I don't know how he did it, except by the grace of God. I never thought that I would look in the mirror with a bald head and know that my husband had more hair than I did! I was filled with anger and humiliation all at the same time. He saw my expression and said, "Hey, one thing's for sure; you have a great bald head." With that comment, I was able to give him a smile and go back to bed.

Right after my ultimate haircut, I went out with my mother, my mother-in-law, and whoever else was up to the chore of shopping for a wig. But I was never able to find a suitable wig that I liked. After I would wear one for a while, I'd start to hate it and would try to change the shape, eventually ruining the wig. Marie talked with my hairdresser, who told her to have me come in with the wigs, and she would style them on me. She was so caring that she even said I could sit in the back room so that no one would see me. I had been going to her shop for at least five years and knew everyone there. I was so angry at the thought of having to go to the back room and get my hair done, or should I say, my wig done, that I refused to go. My anger had nothing to do with my hairdresser. She was so accommodating and wanted to do everything to get me through this. My anger was about my situation and losing my hair.

Not only did I have trouble finding a suitable wig; they were so hot and uncomfortable that I could not stand to wear them. So I started looking for a halo type of wig that only had the edges of hair with the center cut out. The search went on for months, with Marie making every suggestion in the book and me rejecting them, until she did some research and found a place that sold halo wigs. I was ecstatic and could not wait to get there. But when we arrived, there were none for me; they all had gray hair. However, my mom asked if she could look at the halos to get an idea of how to make them, and the lady agreed. I was desperate, and I think they both were sick of me. Mom studied the wigs carefully, and then she used my old cut-up wigs and made halos! She and Auntie Rhena made several of them for me; some were even attached to hats! I was so excited about my new look. The halo wigs with the hats attached gave me much relief in the summer heat. I prayed that my hat would never fall off!

Then I started to have hot flashes. They were brutal, and I said, "Is this what my menopausal patients go through?" However, I could not take estrogen for relief because of the cancer, so I just suffered—one minute hot and the next minute cold. Oh, it was even worse in the winter when I hated waking up with my back all wet and the sheet wet because of the hot flashes. At the same time, it was cold in the room, and I did not want to roll over onto the wet sheets. But I also didn't want to get out of the bed into the cold air so that I could put on dry clothing. I would sweat in places that I didn't even know contained sweat glands. I complained profusely since I could not take anything. Even the herbal medications were not recommended because they can stimulate estrogen receptors—so I just suffered.

Finally, the Lord placed it on my heart that each time I got a hot flash, I should think of Him and how far along He had brought me. God told me to start praising Him because I was still alive with advanced-stage cancer. And although the flashes were still there, I began to praise God for sustaining my life. When I began to do this, it seemed as though I was not so devastated about them—because my focus was on Him instead of me. To this day, when I get a hot flash, not only do I praise God, but I shout out one of His glorious names, such as *Jehovah-Jireh,* the God who provides.

The chemotherapy also caused me to have a mental fog, which is called chemobrain. This made it difficult to remember past events, but mostly I had trouble with present information. As a result, I could not recall a lot of my medical information, and I didn't have the ability to concentrate and read my medical journals. Furthermore, my plans were to never practice medicine again. I almost abhorred medicine; the thought of putting an IV into a patient made me sick.

Another treasure I learned in darkness is: *God has the final say in what you do when you surrender your life to Him.* Though we may go through darkness, He gives us gifts and talents to use, and we are not to waste them. Shortly after I had made this rash decision, during my next chemotherapy visit, a lady was having a reaction to her treatment and started to pass out. They needed a doctor immediately. I went over to evaluate her, and before I even knew what I was doing, I was practicing medicine again, even while receiving chemotherapy through an IV in my arm! I knew this was God telling me not to worry about my memory or the practice of medicine—it would all come back to me.

Overall, my behavior embarrassed me. As a doctor, I felt that I should be able to take the treatments, since I had seen the side effects in my patients during residency when I treated ovarian and cervical cancer patients. But all this flew out the window when I became the patient. In essence, I was the worst patient I had ever seen. After my second treatment, I was such a basket case that I tried to conceal it from Dr. Lusch; I was so ashamed of my behavior. Finally, my husband asked the doctor if he could give me a sedative to calm me down. I really needed something to help me make it into the treatment room and something for the trip home after the chemotherapy.

Being such a kind man, he looked at me with his warm smile and stated, "We doctors who become patients try to stand so firm that we pretend we have no problems, right?" Of course, he said I should be sedated; and he even reduced my chemotherapy dose to try and relieve the symptoms. This helped some, but mostly I had to struggle through the nausea and vomiting after each treatment. Throughout the day, I felt like the dancing girls called "The Rockettes" were doing a jig in my stomach.

To summarize my first four treatments: I would get the chemotherapy for two hours in a room with other cancer patients. And when it was over, I would be nauseated and ready to vomit in the car. They tried all types of antinausea drugs, but none of them worked for me. I had such a bad taste in my mouth from the chemotherapy that I could not eat for seven to ten days. By the eleventh day, my mother would make my favorite foods and I could eat again, only to get ready for another round of treatment. Shereene called me before my second treatment, during one of my down episodes, and I recall her saying, "I did it, Taffy; you can and will get through this with God's help."

In fact, my whole equilibrium was off because of the side effects of the treatments. When I would get up after lying down all day, I would have to sit on the side of the bed and hold my head before I could walk. Then I would hold on to the wall for balance while walking to the bathroom. I would never venture farther than from my bedroom to the bathroom for at least seven days after treatments because of my symptoms. Being the good sport that he is, my poor husband had to sleep on a cot because with the slightest movement in the bed, I would throw up, due to the nausea and my unstable equilibrium.

With each chemotherapy treatment, my symptoms became worse. I had a real problem with odors; everything smelled overwhelmingly strong. When I first met Roland, I loved to smell his cologne. But the odor had become so overbearing that I could not tolerate it; and for my sake, he would put it on in the car. I could not even stand to smell food cooking. And so, to keep me from being disturbed by the odors, my dear mother would have to cook at night while I was sleeping. She is such a good mom; her dedication made me realize what a wonderful, kind, and compassionate mother I have. She would patiently put up with my constant whining.

As she reports, one day when I was feeling better, I called her into the bedroom and told her that I wanted her to bring me some food. To this day I don't remember the conversation, but she does. I have always been a practical joker, and she said that I gave her specific orders on what I wanted, and when she was walking down the stairs from my room, she heard me mumble under my breath, "Chop, chop, and get it done now." My mom turned around and said, "What did you say?" She told me that I had the nerve to repeat it. By then I was laughing hysterically, and said again, "Chop, chop, and get it done now."

Since I was in a playful mood and laughing like crazy, she could not yell at me because she knew that I was only joking. Mom was just glad that I was feeling better—even if it was at her expense. I know that I have the best mother in the world. Roland

and I often comment on how great Mom was for both of us. She took a lot of the burden from him in helping out during this time. Neither he nor Mom ever complained, even though every day I would find something else I could not tolerate.

I suffered not only from the nausea and vomiting but from severe muscle and leg cramps, which are also side effects from the chemotherapy. Then one day, when I had given up on God because I was not getting any relief, my mother-in-law came to see me. I told her, "God has laid me on a shelf and has forgotten about me." She said, "The Devil is a liar." She took some oil and massaged me for nearly two hours and prayed for me. I tell you that I never felt better—it took the soreness out of my legs and arms. I know God can give you what you need and be right on time with it.

On Saturdays, my friend Barb and I would talk. I would look forward to her calls, and she would give me a word from the Lord to console me. My good friend Esther also heard my cries almost daily and always reminded me of the Lord's goodness. She was so compassionate that sometimes I didn't want to tell her things because I knew that she would probably cry when she hung up the phone. Esther hated to see me going through this. She kept telling me that someday I was going to tell this story, and God would use my experience mightily—if I stayed faithful.

I took much comfort from all the cards, gifts, and support from my church family, as well as my family and friends. My niece Danni, whom I adore, is like a daughter to me. While I was in medical school, I spent a lot of time with her and her sister Dionna, whom I'm very close to as well. Danni would send me a card every week with a Scripture she had picked out for me. I would search the mail looking for what she had sent me from the Lord. By God's grace, it would be just what I needed.

I love all of my nieces and nephews; they were so supportive of me throughout this time. Every other day, one after another they would call me, first Dionna, next Carla, then Jade, and Danni, and down the line. I could hear in their voices the love and concern they had for their auntie. When my poor niece Ashley came to see me with her parents, she just cried in my bedroom; she hated so much to see how I was suffering. I tried to do everything that I could to console her and tell her that I was going to be okay, but she was only thirteen at the time and was having difficulty accepting my illness. Even my nephews, John, "G," and JR, would see fit to check on me periodically.

My sister-in-law, Brandon, sent me school pictures of my niece Devon. My two nephews Alex and Chris were so adorable; I remember keeping them at the side of my bed and I'd glance at them when I awoke in the morning. Chris was learning how to write in school and would send Marie, Shereene, and me letters telling us how much he loved us. The three of us would brag about Chris's letters; it even became a competition between us about who received the most endearing letter.

During the chemotherapy treatments, I had a chance to reflect over my life—how I had practiced medicine and had given these same treatments to ovarian cancer patients. In spite of my resolve to give loving care to my oncology patients in residency, and thinking that I was being a compassionate doctor, there were times when I was not. In particular, when the nurse would call me at 2:00 a.m. to come and push their chemotherapy treatment, I would be extremely tired and would hardly talk to them because I was so fatigued from a lack of sleep. I now wish that I had taken more time with them; I should have been more understanding and willing to console them. I now know how they felt. Regardless of whether it was in the middle of the night and how tired I was, I knew what sickness was going to come on them—and they deserved a kind word.

Even after Shereene had breast cancer, I vowed to be more compassionate with cancer patients and their families. I had tried then, but after undergoing this suffering, I still felt that I had a long way to go. I even thought about my obstetrical patients who sometimes had nausea and vomiting throughout the whole pregnancy and couldn't keep anything down. I had some who were put on IV therapy for several months because it was so bad; I now knew what they felt too. After attending to the lady in the chemotherapy room, I vowed that if God allowed me to practice medicine again, I would be a much more considerate doctor in every aspect of care—whether for pregnant women or cancer patients—I would be more sympathetic and sensitive to their needs.

I also started to ponder over the greatest gift that was given to me, which is my salvation in the Lord Jesus Christ and how He died for me. One night I was so sick to my stomach that I thought to myself, *Suppose I suffer like this and do not survive this cancer?* Then I thought about how my suffering could not compare with the suffering Jesus endured to save me from my sins. He was highly afflicted and did nothing wrong. He was God and went through such terrible agony to be the supreme sacrifice so that I could spend eternity with Him. It became clearer to me that, as Jesus' suffering was not in vain, God also had a purpose for my suffering.

God allowed me these thoughts to help me put things into perspective. I could now see that only pure goodness came out of Jesus' suffering for me. As a result, I have become eternally grateful and have never looked at the cross again without realizing what a great sacrifice He made for me. The year before my cancer I had been meditating on Philippians 3:10, *"That I may know him, and the power of his resurrection, and the fellowship of his sufferings, being made conformable unto his death."* Little did I know at the time that God was going to answer my prayer to know Him through this Scripture and my encounter with the disease of breast cancer.

After the four courses of chemotherapy, the tumor had shrunk, but not enough to warrant a lumpectomy. There was a good response to the treatments, but breast conservation was not going to be for me. The tumor was still too large to get clear margins around the cancer. Therefore, I knew when Dr. Lusch sent me back to my surgeon she was going to say that I needed a mastectomy.

Yes, I was still asking God to shrink the tumor, or make it go completely away with the chemotherapy, so that I would not have to have surgery. But this time I was praying for a miracle and also actively getting the treatment that the doctor recommended. If God saw fit to reduce the tumor so that I wouldn't need a mastectomy—then great. But if He did not, I was still moving in the direction of His will and would proceed with the mastectomy. I was not going to stop treatment and dictate to Him. If He saw fit not to shrink the tumor entirely, then I would go forward with my surgery.

Through the storm of chemotherapy treatments that I endured, I was starting to grow in the Lord and surrender to His will for my life. I was learning to let go of my own desires and what I thought was best for me. This is the process the Lord took me through to teach me that His will is sovereign and supersedes my own desires. It showed me how to be obedient to God and accept the fact that it was still not in God's will to heal me supernaturally. Another treasure I learned in darkness is: *The more obedient you are to God, the more He will show you His will.*

Looking back at all the sickness that I suffered during my chemotherapy, some people might wonder if it is worth the trouble to endure the pain. Many cancer patients are prone to stop, throw in the towel, and cease all their treatments at this time because it is difficult. This is understandable since there were days when I said, "I'm not going on," and I meant it. But the reason I went forward was that I knew God was directing me to continue on in the therapy. Moreover, my husband and family were such an immense support to me. When I wanted to give up, they were right there to offer the words of encouragement that I needed to help me continue.

Shereene and my aunt Rhena would call me. I knew that they were aware of what I was going through, and, somehow, after talking with them and knowing God had brought them through, it really seemed to get me ready for my next treatment. But I cannot emphasize enough that it was God, and Him alone, who would comfort me in the darkest nights when I was not only sick, but lonely too. These were times when I felt no one else knew my true despair. God would give me the guiding treasures of how to make it through this storm and keep on going. God's powerful promises became so valuable to me, such as, *"I will never leave you or forsake you"* (Hebrews 13:5), *"My grace is sufficient for you"* (2 Corinthians 12:9), and many others as well. Jesus is *the* Rock, and I learned to depend on Him throughout many weak moments and troubled days. Although I call my husband a rock, and truly he was supportive of me, I learned as the songwriter said, "Jesus is a rock in a weary land."

There may be some of you out there who are going through the adversity of breast cancer right now and are ready to give up the fight. I encourage you not to give up. Even if you do not have a great support system, know that if you reach out to Jesus, He can and will be that friend who sticks closer to you than a brother. All you have to do is call on Him and He will be there for you.

If you do have a great support person—a husband, mother, sister, or others, always remember that God has placed them in your life and they should be appreciated to the utmost. But no one will be able to comfort you like the Lord. He allows these storms in our lives so that we will know His unfailing love and His ability to comfort us through His mighty power. God and God alone is able to provide for our needs as the Scripture asserts in Philippians 4:19, *"But my God shall supply all your need according to his riches in glory by Christ Jesus."* When you learn to depend on Him, Jesus can fill all of your needs more than any person could ever do. Call on Jesus and believe in your heart that He is able; then watch the presence of God become very real in your situation. I know that this is true because of my own need for His comfort and healing, which He saw fit to provide for me during my trial of affliction.

Treasure

God and only God is the source of your comfort. He may put individuals in your path to comfort you, but know that they are sent from God. There are some who do not have those human comforters and are going through the storm right now. That does not mean God has forgotten you. Oh, no, it just means that His hand will be there to comfort you—if you just let Him in.

6

MASTECTOMY: "OKAY, I SURRENDER"

I went off to surgery not really sure what I was feeling about having a mastectomy at that time. I was so used to seeing my patients who had breast cancer that it was not going to be a shock to me what the scar and aftereffects were going to look like. I'm sure I had some emotion about my breast being removed, but it was not until afterward when I looked in the mirror that it really hit me. Before my surgery, I had finally accepted that the mass was big. Although the chemotherapy had shrunk it quite a bit, it was still there—and I wanted it removed. Therefore, I was ready for the mastectomy.

However, I was more worried about the complications from the surgery. Being a surgeon, I knew what could happen during a surgical process. Shortly before the operation, either that morning or the night before, I sat my husband down and told him that I was not going to make it out of surgery; in fact, I was sure of it. I was aware of all the things that could go wrong, from complications with the anesthesia right down to the actual procedure. Being the rock of stability that he is, my husband looked me square in the face and said, "I hear what you are saying, and I do not discount that you know what to expect from surgery; but I know what God has told me about your healing, and I stand firm on this." He never wrote off my medical knowledge, but he always pointed me to a higher authority—to the One who is in charge and has the final say—which is God. To this day, I call him a rock because he never strays from the Word of God when giving advice. With that confident assurance, I never said another word about possible complications, and I prepared myself for the coming event.

My surgery went remarkably well, and so did my recovery. I was only in the hospital for twenty-four hours. Roland told me that my surgeon came out after the operation with a big smile and said, "Everything went well." She was glad that the tumor had shrunk significantly with the four courses of preoperative chemotherapy. That report on her behavior was interesting to me since we always knew her as a very stern but caring doctor, who showed very little emotion when she spoke. But aside from her usually stern demeanor, she was able to express such a warm concern that showed how much she really cares for her patients.

After the operation, Roland was waiting in my hospital room. When they brought me in from the recovery room, he was so elated that my surgery had gone well, he ran to embrace me as the nurses were getting ready to transfer me from the stretcher to the hospital bed. However, he said that I lifted up my head, and when I saw him, I said, "Where's Mommy?" My husband told me that he felt like chopped liver and wanted to respond, "What about me; am I not good enough? I'm your husband." But he knew that I had been through a great ordeal over the last three months. And besides, I was looking pretty glassy eyed from the anesthesia. If my mom was the first person I wanted to see, that was okay with him, as long as I was all right—and I was.

Perhaps I had asked for Mom because of the fond memories I have from times when I was sick as a child. My mother is an excellent nurse. She would stay home with me until I got well, and she would feed me in my room. When I had the measles, she cooked my favorite foods, and I got to stay up late and watch TV. For about three months since my diagnosis, Mom had been living with us and taking care of me. Sometimes anesthesia can make you say funny things.

Roland stayed all night with me in my hospital room, sitting up in the chair adjacent to me. I would doze off and wake up; we would talk for a few minutes, and then I would go back to sleep. That evening, Mom, Marie, and my nieces all came to see me. I remember someone trying to feed me some Jell-O, but Danni later told me that I refused it. I said that I wanted "Mommy" to feed me. I must have really reverted to my childhood. Mom had said to them before they came into the hospital room, "No tears." They later told me that when Marie saw me, she ran into the other room crying, and said "Lord, please help my sister. There has to be a better way than this to deliver her from breast cancer." She hated to see me like this, bald and now with only one breast. Marie and I share a lot with each other. We could not know then that we would also share in the experience of having the same disease.

After I had healed from my mastectomy, I went to see Dr. Lusch again to discuss my further treatments. I had two positive lymph nodes out of six; therefore, he recommended a total of four courses of chemotherapy instead of the planned two. He explained how this would be a different chemotherapy and would probably not be as harsh. But just as before, I wanted no part of it. After surgery, my hair had just started to grow back during the six weeks without chemotherapy. It was growing in a completely different texture. To my surprise and my husband's, it was now soft and fine; whereas before it was coarse and curly. He liked it so much that he started calling me "Baby Hair." He even had some of the church members calling me "Baby Hair." I would just chuckle at my new name. So, of course, I did not want any more chemotherapy than the planned two on which I had already set my mind. My nails were getting back their color; the chemotherapy had caused them to turn black because the cytotoxic drugs attack the good cells as well as the cancerous cells in the body. I was no longer having nausea and vomiting; and I could even walk better, though I still had pain in my joints and legs. But all in all, I was coming to life again. Spring had arrived and the trees were blossoming. The birds were singing, and I felt better. I had a shred of hope that my treatments were soon coming to an end.

When I went to see my surgeon for a postoperative checkup

from the mastectomy, she said that my scar was healing very well. So I asked her when she thought I could have reconstructive surgery. As we discussed my future, she reminded me of my two positive lymph nodes. She did not recommend it until six months after completion of my treatments because I needed healing from all my treatments. Also, because of the size of the tumor, there was a high risk of recurrence in the first year. I went home discouraged, thinking, *If I'm going to die, I might as well die now rather than go through all those treatments.* I became so distraught that I told the Lord to take me then. It felt like the day I had been diagnosed with cancer. I felt alone, but knew that I was not alone; Jesus was with me. My husband was out of the country, so I could not readily reach him. Furthermore, I did not want to upset my mom and my sisters. Feeling alone and extremely sad, I just sat in my study and cried.

The surgeon was right and needed to tell me the truth. I recalled having to be blunt with patients regarding their potential outcomes of treatments and survivals, and she was only telling me the truth from a statistical standpoint. My chances for survival were not good based on my advanced stage. There was no need to rush into major surgery for cosmetic purposes until we were certain that I was going to survive at least the first year. I turned to the book of Psalms for comfort as I had started to do during my illness. The Lord gave me an encouraging word from Psalm 90:10, *"The days of our years are threescore years and ten; and if by reason of strength they be fourscore years . . . "* This verse leaped off the page and spoke right to my spirit. I said, "God is talking to me!" I dropped to my knees and thanked God for the Word of truth; for it supersedes my knowledge of medicine and those dreary statistics that I knew all too well.

Later that evening, I was still in my study reading the Bible, praying, and talking with God. My husband called and I told him what happened; he immediately responded, "God has the final say about life and death." He recalled what God had told him the week I was diagnosed, and he was resting on God's promises. Roland prayed for me over the phone, and I told him that God had given me the Scripture in Psalm 90. He said that was one of his father's favorite verses. He reminded me that God is faithful and will be true to His promises. I then realized that it was not meant for anyone to be in my study that day to console me. How else would I have ever pored over the Word of God looking for an answer to my sorrow? I was even able to thank God for allowing me to be on the receiving end to hear how it sounds to be a statistic.

Now I am very sensitive when it comes to telling people about statistics without telling them about God as well. I still praise God and meditate on this Scripture anytime I'm afraid of dying or of the cancer coming back. When I go for my check-ups and have my blood work done, I think of this Scripture to prepare me for anything that I might hear. I now know that the end of my life is in His hands. I will never forget this season when God spoke clearly to me through His Word in one of the darkest times of my life. This was another treasure I learned in darkness: *God can either speak directly to your spirit, or He can speak to you through His Word—and be right on time.*

My four courses of postoperative chemotherapy with the cytotoxic drug Taxotere resulted in another round of fatigue, muscle aches, and weakness, but not much nausea. I was able to eat, and I started to gain weight. My hair fell out again; but overall, compared to the first four courses of preoperative chemotherapy with Adriamycin and Cytoxan, I did much better and had fewer side effects. The only real problem I had was the extreme fatigue accompanied by muscle and joint pain.

In between treatments, I was able to travel with Marie to Washington, D.C., when she dropped her daughter, Jade, at Georgetown University for a college preparatory summer program. Marie thought this would be a great cultural experience for Jade, which would allow her to see the museums and all the cultural events that Washington has to offer. There were students from all over the world participating in the program. In fact, we both felt Jade needed to branch out and see the world a bit and be exposed to other cultures before she enrolled in college. She was a "mommy's girl" who loved to stick very close to her mom. Jade had attended private schools all her life and was very sheltered. At that time she was in the tenth grade at an all girls' school.

While she was there, my brother Jay, who lived in Washington, could keep an eye on her. He met us on campus. We moved Jade into her dorm room and introduced ourselves to her roommate, who was from overseas. Marie and I both had also once lived in Washington; and on the ride down, we told Jade there were certain areas we did not want her to visit in Washington. She asked about Dupont Circle in particular, and we said to stay away from that area; it had a reputation for trouble.

A few weeks after I returned home, I ventured out to the

airport to pick up my girlfriend Jean. I had already received my second treatment, and she was coming to visit. As I drove along, Roland phoned to tell me that my brother Jay had suffered a heart attack. In shock from the news, I responded, "No way; I just saw Jay and didn't notice any problems." I immediately became fearful of losing my dear Jay. I could not believe this was happening. I started to feel numb, and for a moment I really thought that I was dreaming. But the reality of being behind the wheel forced me to steady myself enough to continue driving.

My husband and my sister Marie were already en route to Washington, D.C. He thought that maybe I should remain at home until they reached Washington and could give me more information. He was not sure if I was up for the trip with the new chemotherapy that I was getting. I told him that I would pick Jean up and ask her to drive me down to Washington. This made me extremely anxious to greet Jean; and as soon as she got into the car, I blurted out the news about Jay. I could see the shock on her face as she responded, "Let's go." As soon as we reached my home, I quickly packed a bag and headed back to Washington. God knows whom to put with you at a time of crisis. I thank God that Jean was with me; all the way to Washington, she spoke words of encouragement to me. Moreover, during this time of emergency, I quietly thanked God that I wasn't feeling as bad as I had felt with the first chemotherapy.

Another treasure I learned in darkness is: *God is able to see you through anything He places in your path.* By His strength, we are able to endure the circumstances that we face when we rest on God's Word. Philippians 4:13 (NKJV) assured me, *"I can do all things through Christ who strengthens me.* " By the Son of God who resides in me, I was able to speak with the doctors concerning Jay's medical condition and to assist in his recovery for two weeks. However, when Jay was about to go into surgery, I went into the restroom and just cried. Jay and I are so close, and my dear brother has been the backbone of our entire family.

Each one of us knew while Jay was lying in that hospital bed that we had all contributed to his condition. Through all the stress and strain—emotional, financial, and physical—Jay had always been there for us, ever since we were children. Even as adults, some of us were still very dependant on Jay. My family members were right there, as we all should have been. At least twenty of us were crowded into his room before he went off to surgery, to show our love and support. I was aware that the bypass surgery needed to be done, and we needed it to be successful.

At that time, God gave me this Scripture, *"For the battle is not yours, but God's"* (2 Chronicles 20:15). I definitely saw this as a battle for Jay's life. But God showed me, though I viewed this as a battle, and I knew all about medicine, I could not cure Jay. The battle did not belong to me—it belonged to the Lord. At that moment in the restroom, I surrendered Jay to God. I said, "Yes, Lord, this battle is not mine, and I surrender it to You." Before Jay went off to surgery, in his room we kept playing softly the song, "The Battle Is Not Yours but the Lord's" by Yolanda Adams. Jay and all of us were comforted as we prayed and read Scriptures to him. As we trusted in the Lord and cried out to Him on behalf of Jay in this way, it made me realize how we all had grown closer to the Lord over the last few years.

Here was yet another opportunity for me to see God's healing power working in my family. God brought Jay safely through the surgery and healed his body by the surgeons placing seven new vessels in his heart. Jay's heart was pumping so loudly that one night he called the nurse into the room and asked why they were doing construction in the hospital in the middle of the night. A very wise and confident nurse responded, "That is not construction you are hearing; it is your new heart pumping blood."

I praise God for His goodness and the healing power that He demonstrated in Jay's life. I am fully persuaded that—in spite of the doctors and surgeons being involved in Jay's care—it was God who used them to heal Jay, and the credit belongs to God. By the grace of God, Jay did very well;, and I was back in Philadelphia two weeks later, ready for my next chemotherapy session.

Another highlight of that trip to Washington, if I may say that it was, occurred when Shereene, Marie, my niece Carla, my nephew "G," and I went to pick up my nephew John from work one evening. John worked near Dupont Circle, and while we were waiting for him, Shereene screamed out, "There's Jade!" Marie said, "No way. Jade is in the library, and we told her not to hang out around here." Marie had just mentioned before we left that Jade was a little down, and we were going to pick her up for dinner later.

Shereene said again, "I know my niece, and that is Jade!" We all looked closely, and it was Jade! Not only was it Jade, but she wore a do-rag on her head, like the rappers do. Some parts of her hair were sticking straight up like a punk rocker's, and she had on the tightest designer cropped pants we had ever seen her wear. And to top it off, all we could see were her hips rocking from side to side as she walked. We were not only surprised to see her in a place where we had told her not to go, but we were even more astonished by her outfit! My quiet, very shy niece, who dressed in a very conservative and modest manner up until now, shocked us when we saw her overnight transformation. Not to mention that she was supposed to be depressed, and we were going to have dinner with her that night to cheer her up!

We sent her brother "G" to go and get her, and when she came to the car, she said, "Hi, Mom." Marie replied, "Don't 'hi, Mom' me. I told you not to hang out around here. And what do you have on?" We all laughed hysterically about Jade's outfit. Jade had no idea what we were laughing about, so finally Marie said she would talk with her later, because she saw that we were not making the situation any better. Finally, her cousin John said, in the voice of Darth Vader (from *Star Wars*), "Jade, we see you; we are your family, and we are everywhere!" He then closed up the car window while looking at her with a long and slow glare. We all laughed again and couldn't believe that John had done this to frighten her; he was acting as if we had been following her.

We all laughed so hard that we forgot to scold her about being at Dupont Circle. Her mom did have a word with her later that evening. However, we were all so seriously drained from Jay's heart attack and so focused on his situation, this was the emotional break that we needed at the time. Marie and I still tease Jade about her drastic makeover. Thank God, she has since returned to earth. We were never sure if she even made it to the museums and the cultural events, but we were sure of one thing—it was truly a cultural experience for her and for us!

By God's grace, I made it through the mastectomy and the first three courses of postoperative chemotherapy with Taxotere. I also saw the healing power of God work through Jay's heart attack—all within three months. Though I was exhausted and emotionally drained then, I know God is real and can sustain you through not only your storm but the storms of your loved ones as well—if you surrender all things, including your loved ones, over to Him.

Treasure

God is able to see you through any situation that He places in your path. According to Philippians 4:13, Christ gives us the strength to endure the trials that come our way.

RADIATION THERAPY: "IT'S ALMOST OVER"

Back from Washington, by the grace of God, I made it through my last round of chemotherapy and started six weeks of radiation therapy. Radiation involves the use of radioactive electrons, or beams, directed at the cancer cells to kill the cancerous tissue. For the most part, the actual process of radiation is painless in the treatment of breast cancer. I was placed in a dark room to lie down as a beam of light was directed at the area to be radiated, which happened to be my bare chest wall. The treatments occurred daily for five days and lasted five to ten minutes for a six week period. This process was chosen for me because the size of my tumor was so large and close to my chest wall. These facts not only increased the chance of recurrence at my surgical scar, but the possibility of not getting all the cancer cells at the mastectomy site was also heightened. So they wanted to radiate my remaining chest wall to be certain no cancer cells were left to multiply.

I met the team consisting of exceptionally pleasant people who conducted a simulation procedure that took about one hour. One of the team members marked me with a pen and placed the radiation beam over the area where I would have the treatment. Using a solid material and following the marks, an imprint of my chest wall was made. When the material was removed, the imprint was used to simulate what they were going to do in the actual treatment. They told me not to wipe off the pen marks until the next visit in case the imprint did not take and the process would need to be repeated.

When I left, I looked pretty silly with those black marks on my neck. In the midst of the summer heat, I tried to hide them with a scarf. I remembered as a medical student seeing patients walking around the hospital with markings on their necks; it was always a sure sign that they had cancer or were receiving radiation for some other serious disease. The marks seemed to say, "Look at me; I have cancer." And I always felt so sorry for them. Now I was one of them.

While going through radiation therapy, I would recognize the people in the waiting room, since the visits are scheduled for the same time every day. The patients ranged from young women, at the least in their thirties, to older men in their seventies. As we all sat there day after day waiting for our names to be called, we got to know one another. It was very discouraging for me to see women younger than myself battling this disease. For instance, there was a young teacher who appeared to be in her thirties. She looked so frail and thin but was continuing to teach her students throughout her treatments, in spite of being very ill from the chemotherapy. She felt this would be a good life lesson for them to learn—that we can survive the adversities in life.

This brave young woman told me that she and her students wrote in their journals about her plight with breast cancer. They described how the treatments made her ill with nausea, vomiting, and serious weight loss. She had also taken off her wig to show them the loss of her hair. The students were aware that her absence from class meant that she was sick following one of her treatments. Yet she courageously hoped to show them the victory in the end when she was finally finished with her treatments and cured of the disease.

I think the children were either in the third or fourth grade, and I agreed that this would teach them a great deal about life. It was just incredible to me that she could be so strong, and I certainly commended her on her determination to help others through her pain. I thought to myself, *She is definitely turning this cancer situation into good for the sake of others.*

After my simulation that day, I attended the funeral of one of our church members. I felt so guilty that I had survived cancer and he had not. David was only in his early twenties and had been battling cancer since he was a teenager. He had received at least ten rounds of chemotherapy from the time of his diagnosis —and God still called him home. At his young age, David was such a great witness for the Lord. He would encourage me through the cards and songs that he offered during my illness.

He would call and tell me, "You will get by because you are blessed that a lot of research has been done in breast cancer." He also said, "God will see us both through this thing."

David kept the faith right to the very end; he never gave up on the Lord. Even when the cancer was so advanced that you could see it coming through his temples, he always had a positive outlook and believed in God. When I saw him, I could not imagine how he could be so upbeat. David would also encourage my husband, who was so proud of this young man, and was in endless prayer for him. So needless to say, I didn't want him to go. At the funeral, my husband, though with a heavy heart, preached one of the most powerful sermons I have ever heard. We all left the funeral knowing that David is in heaven. We also have the hope that we will meet him again.

Through all of these events, I couldn't help but notice that I was beginning to feel depressed. At the time, I was going for my daily radiation therapy, and I found myself looking forward to visiting with the technicians who were giving the treatments. They would offer me a caring word or a smile that would really lift my spirits, and they always had another story to tell me about their families. They would keep me in stitches talking about their husbands and their children. When the session was over, I really wished it wasn't, as I was starting to have joy again. I was learning to laugh in spite of what I was going through. God was working through these ladies to minister to me. I told Beth, one of the technicians, that I was grateful for her kind spirit. Even though this was a difficult time for me, she made it easier to cope with the situation. The treasure I learned here in darkness is: *God is faithful, and He can use anyone He chooses to minister to our needs.*

So when my radiation therapy ended, it was a sad thing for me because I knew that I would miss the uplifting visits I had been having. But, thank God, I really didn't have any side effects, except for a minor case of sunburn. However, even with the sunburn, my skin did not slough off. One of the most detrimental effects can be a serious sunburn, which can cause a delay in the treatments until the area improves. In these cases, severe skin irritation occurs and the skin sloughs off. Sometimes radiation causes side effects that are not apparent until two to six months after treatment has been completed. For example, a few months after treatment, a patient may experience pain and hardening of the chest wall, called radiation fibrosis, which can last several years and interfere with reconstructive surgery. As a result, the radiated tissue usually never looks the same as before. I truly thank God for giving me favor and not allowing me to experience a serious degree of side effects such as these.

One week after I finished my treatments, I was on my way to Florida to see my dad. Dad was becoming more debilitated from arthritis. Even though Mom and Dad had been divorced for several years, my mother is a jewel and had agreed to take my dad to live with her in Florida. He was moving from Detroit where he had been living with my brother. But Dad's health was deteriorating, and it was becoming more difficult to take care of him. The best option for him was to move in with my mom for a time, since her house was equipped for handicapped persons, and Dad was now confined to a wheelchair.

Mom had just returned home to Florida from nursing me

back to health for six months, and two weeks later she had gone to Washington to help nurse Jay back to health after his heart attack. Needless to say, we knew that she was tired, but we had to ask her if she would help. When we asked, she wanted to think about it and let us know the next morning. I knew Mom was praying about it; she always prayed before every decision. She called as promised and said that she would take Dad. We were grateful to God; this was really a blessing for us all. I remember praying throughout that night, asking God that if this was the right thing to do, He would make it clear to her—which He did. I truly know that I have a godly mother, mostly because of her love for God and her willingness to follow His leading in her life.

While I was in Florida, our women's ministry held a retreat in Tampa. There were at least forty-five of us who came down from Philadelphia. We had such a great time, laughing and sharing about our lives. Our joy was interspersed with tears of pain from past failures we had experienced by doing things our own way and not trusting in the Lord. This was a time of cleansing that brought a spiritual renewal for us all. It was a wonderful time in the Lord, and that was just what I needed. I had been unable to attend church or the monthly women's fellowship lunches throughout most of my illness. However, during this retreat, the women gave me such comfort and love that it made me realize how much they love me and how much I had missed them.

After returning from Florida and seeing that Dad was settled in, I started my recovery phase. There was no need to think about returning to work because I was too physically and mentally exhausted to do the work of an OB/GYN. I was suffering from fatigue due to the combination of chemotherapy, radiation treatments, and traveling. I could hardly walk. The last rounds of postoperative chemotherapy with Taxotere had really caused my muscles and joints to ache. So I told myself that I would take six months to heal from all my treatments, and then I would proceed with reconstructive surgery. My plan was to have a brief period of recovery to allow all of the radiation changes to take place before my reconstruction; I would then be in a better position to handle the surgery. However, God had another plan that was about to unfold.

Treasure

God is a faithful God who uses people and our circumstances to show us His goodness—in spite of what we may be going through. Our responsibility is to look to Him in these circumstances and develop a relationship with Him. We must not turn away from Him, but run to Him during this time. To quote my husband Roland in one of his great sermons, "Can we not trust the One who died for us?"

RECOVERY PHASE: "OH, NO, NOT MARIE!"

One month into my recovery phase, I had started to enjoy life again. I was sleeping better, the hot flashes were fewer, and I was able to pray and read my Bible more. Up until now, I had been suffering from chemobrain, a condition that makes mental concentration and reading comprehension very difficult. But I was finding out that I could read and meditate on the Word of God again. To my extreme delight, I also began noticing an overwhelming sense that God's presence was with me.

Although my body still ached from the effects of the chemotherapy, I could walk around my yard and take short walks in our woods with my dog, Ramsey. Ramsey was so happy that I was feeling better, because when I was sick I could no longer walk him in our woods. Prior to my illness, every morning before I went off to work and every evening when I returned home, I would take him for long walks. He loved walking and smelling all the different flowers and chasing the deer, raccoons, and rabbits.

After I became ill, Ramsey would bang against the door for my mother or husband to walk him, but they never walked him as far as I did. I would let him take his time and sniff all the smells the woods had to offer. Now that I was feeling better, he would go to the door and stare at me as if to say, *Hey, I know you are better, so let's go!* During our walks, I would talk with the Lord and praise Him for all the wonderful signs of His creation. I enjoyed watching the animals in their natural habitat and observing the many varieties of flowers, such as the lovely marigolds. Of course, there was the beautiful sight to behold when the trees would change their leaves in season. In fact, autumn is my favorite time for walking, when the rust-and yellow-colored leaves fall gracefully from the trees.

We have brooks and streams in our woods, where I would observe the turtles and frogs and even the snakes. Once I saw a large snapping turtle meandering along his way. Although I was able to resume my walks, though I couldn't walk as far as before, I enjoyed watching Ramsey take off and then look back to see if I could catch him. I walked more slowly, but I was very pleased to know that I could do some of my old routines. Best of all, I could talk to the Lord and feel God's presence once again.

Two months into my recovery phase, I got a call from my middle sister, Marie. She said, "I had an abnormal breast exam. The mammogram is normal, but my surgeon is sending me for an MRI." I told her not to worry because God was not going to let her go through the same thing Shereene and I had gone through. Besides, Jay had recently suffered a heart attack, and Mom had gone back to Florida to take care of Dad. There was no way God was going to allow this to happen! Nevertheless, I knew that the situation needed prayer. Since I had joined our women's Bible study group, I asked them to pray for this situation privately. My husband and I were also praying. I was certain that God was not going to put our family through anything else this year. After all, didn't we need a break?

Another treasure I kept relearning in the darkness: *You cannot dictate to God what He will or will not allow to happen. Nor should you tell another person what God will not do in their lives, because God is sovereign, and there is no way for you to be sure.* I was doing exactly what I had accused others of doing when I was diagnosed with my illness. Although I did not want Marie to have breast cancer, God had another plan, and I had to accept this. But when I received the phone call that the MRI was suspicious for cancer and the breast biopsy was positive for cancer, I immediately sank into the worst depression I could ever imagine. I was devastated and did not understand what God was doing. Before this news, I had felt His presence so strongly, but now I could not feel His presence at all. However, having to face this situation forced me to step out on faith just to know that God was there. And my walk with Him became even stronger because I had to see my sister go through the same disease I had just survived.

I soon began to realize that all of these changes were a part of my learning to rely on my faith in God. And I started to depend more on His promises than on my feelings or emotions. I thanked God that I was better able to read His Word and attend church again. This allowed me the opportunity for the Word of God to speak directly to me, and I drew on divine strength to deal with Marie's situation. Through His Word, God was preparing me for this. My mind was becoming clearer, and I was ready to put on my doctor's hat again so that God could use me to orchestrate her care. I recall now that this was when I really started to learn to walk by faith in times of adversity. I even began to see Marie's healing and had a more positive outlook than when either Shereene or I were diagnosed.

As I contemplated Marie's situation, I reflected on the time when I was having my chemotherapy. I was always afraid to go for another treatment because I would get so sick. One day when they asked me to hold out my arm for the IV, I pointed to my husband and said, "Give it to him." He looked at me with such love and compassion and said, "If I could take this for you and even take it away so you don't have to have it, I would. But you must do this because someone in your family may have to go through this, and you will be able to help them cope with it." Little did I know that it would be Marie he was talking about!

Unlike me, Marie surrendered to God immediately by saying, "Whatever You want me to do, Lord, I will do." The only thing she pleaded with God about was that she wanted no chemotherapy. She had recent memories of how sick I was during my chemotherapy treatments and also remembered Shereene's battle with it. Even so, she did say to God, "If that is Your will, I will do it." As a result, Marie was quite certain that she was not going to be any different. In fact, she said this to Shereene when she found out about her abnormal breast exam. But Shereene told her not to worry. And Marie responded, "Why should I be any different from you, Taffy, and Auntie?"

I have always found it interesting that the three of us, along with one of our dearest aunts, all developed breast cancer. My sisters and I are also very close to our mother, and I believe the only reason Mom has not developed breast cancer is because her ovaries had been removed at a young age. This is just a theory and has no scientific basis; however, I cannot help but wonder how four very close women within the same family, who share a lot of their lives together, all ended up sharing the same disease as well. Is it related to our closeness? Perhaps it is due to the tight relationship we have; and in watching the sorrow and pain we saw in one another, something was triggered in our immune systems to react in a way that made us susceptible to the disease as well. These are only possibilities, but I do know that Marie had firsthand knowledge by watching me suffer for eight months. And as soon as I finished my treatments, immediately she was diagnosed with breast cancer—and she wasn't even surprised.

God answered Marie's prayer; she did not need any chemotherapy since she was diagnosed very early. In fact, what she had was ductal carcinoma in situ (DCIS), which is considered stage-zero breast cancer, meaning it is cancer that has not spread beyond the capsule of the milk ducts; that is, not into the surrounding breast tissue. When Marie saw the breast cancer oncology specialist at the University of Pennsylvania, she made it clear to Marie that, although this was breast cancer, it had been caught very early—stage-zero breast cancer. In most cases, a lumpectomy would suffice. However, not in her case, since she already had two sisters who had invasive breast cancer and DCIS. As a result, Marie had had the extreme potential to develop invasive breast cancer. The oncology specialist recommended not only a mastectomy on the affected breast, but stated that she needed a bilateral mastectomy to reduce her risk of getting subsequent invasive breast cancer.

I knew Marie's surgeon very well and had referred many patients to her. When I spoke with her regarding Marie's treatment, we both agreed with the specialist from the University of Pennsylvania that Marie needed a bilateral mastectomy, because she was now the third sister diagnosed with cancer. She would perform the surgery and arrange for Marie to see a plastic surgeon for breast reconstruction. Although we did not want Marie to go through this ordeal, we both agreed that because it was carcinoma in situ (meaning it had not spread out into the breast tissue), removing both breasts should be a cure for her. This may have seemed aggressive, but it would limit the potential for any new cancer to develop in the future.

The only concern the oncologist at the University of Pennsylvania had was that this might possibly be a hurried decision to have both breasts removed at the same time. For emotional considerations, she thought Marie should wait six months to have the second mastectomy. It can be a very devastating situation to cope with having breast cancer and then to also be faced with having a bilateral mastectomy. A woman may not be emotionally ready to deal with the overall trauma this may cause. We all assured her that Marie would be fine; she had not only empathized with Shereene and me and what we had endured, but she had almost been waiting—or should we say, God had been preparing her to handle this situation. I never saw Marie so surrendered and ready to deal with whatever God was telling her to do.

Nevertheless, it was a trying time for all of us. Within just a few months of finishing my treatments, we had seen yet another family member stricken with the same disease. But, thank God, Marie did exceedingly well throughout her ordeal. She underwent a bilateral mastectomy, which was followed by her having permanent implants placed six months later. She also had her ovaries removed later that year. In the event her cancer was hereditary, the risk for ovarian cancer would decrease.

Mom came back to assist with Marie's recovery. And Marie's husband, Gerald, was a great support to her. I remember Gerald calling me one day after Marie and I had returned from the plastic surgeon to discuss her surgery. He asked me if she was going to have any breasts. He understood the mastectomies, but things were moving very fast, and Marie had not had a chance to tell him about our visit that afternoon to the plastic surgeon to discuss her reconstructive surgery. He said it really did not matter to him if she did not ever have breasts again; he was going to love her just the same. I thought this was so endearing of him, and I explained that she would have reconstruction and be all right.

As his pastor, my husband, who is a rock of faith, was able to offer Gerald words of encouragement. But as my caregiver, he also had firsthand knowledge of what Gerald was going through, and had been an excellent support to me. Roland told him that God was faithful and would see him and Marie through, as He had us. By the grace of God, Roland always knows how to point you to the true and living God in the time of crisis. I guess that is why God made him a pastor, and that is why I think of him as a rock. Through it all, Marie did very well, and was probably the best patient of us all. My mother will never tell us who was the best, but I know Shereene and I were definitely a challenge.

Marie and Gerald have three wonderful children. They are very close to their children, their children adore them, and they all know the Lord. However, when Marie was diagnosed with breast cancer they were not sure how their children were going to respond, even though Marie and Gerald assured them they themselves were trusting the Lord through this difficult time.

Jermaine was twenty-six and living on his own. After his initial reaction of shock and disbelief he was able to not only support his mother, but saw that his dad needed encouragement too. He said he would call his dad regularly to check on his emotional well-being, and if Dad wanted to talk about the situation, he would let him talk. Jermaine seemed to handle it very well.

Jade, who was a sixteen-year-old high school junior, did not care to discuss the situation or even face what was happening. It was too emotional for her to process. The mere thought of her mother having breast cancer was upsetting to her. When it came time for Jade to go to the hospital that evening after Marie's surgery, she could not bring herself to go. However, the next day she mustered up enough courage. Though she felt as if her heart would break, she held back her tears and went to the hospital. When Marie saw her she sat up in bed and gave her a warm smile. "Hi Jade," she said. All Jade could manage were a few words. She had difficulty holding back the tears, and she did not want her mother to see her cry, so she sat in the waiting area for the remainder of the visit. When you ask Jade, now twenty-one, how she had the courage to come to the hospital that day, she'll tell you she said to herself, "This is not about me. I need to get there" and support her mom—pretty remarkable for a sixteen-year-old.

"G" is the youngest, fourteen at the time. He was very sad but did not believe his mom would die. He started learning to depend on his faith. He said that not once could he picture his mom dying. He took comfort in remembering how I had made it through the ordeal as did Shereene, and he had faith his mom was going to be all right too. He visited the hospital and I remember him sitting on his mom's bed talking to her as if everything was okay. He had such a brave look on his face. You could not tell he was hurting, until that evening he and I came home to Marie's house. I kept asking him things like, "Where's the toothpaste?" and "I need a toothbrush." As he looked for these items he got frustrated and finally turned to me and burst out sadly, "Auntie, I don't know where any of this stuff is; Mom does all this for me!" Right then I knew how much he was hurting and I just prayed silently that God would comfort him in his sleep that night because I knew he missed his mom. Today "G" says to other children who might be going through a similar experience, "It's not in your hands, just have faith."

Children who are faced with a parent who has cancer will respond in different ways. Some may appear to handle it and can discuss it openly, and others may shy away and not want to talk about it because it is so painful. Each child is different and we must respect these differences and trust in God's ability to see them through the situation. What Marie and Gerald did was bring God into the circumstances and teach their children how He can see you through a storm. It can be a great learning tool for the entire family as they all go through it together. We should not try to make one child's response be like another's. Each child is made individually and has an unique set of emotions. Yes, discuss their fears with them, if they so desire, but if they don't, maybe someone else you trust will get them to open up. God knows their needs best.

Now that Marie was settled in after her surgery, the rush was over, and I had time to reflect on what had just happened. I praised God over and over again that her breast cancer was caught early and she would be cured with the surgery. The statistics of her survival would be much better than mine since she was diagnosed early. I am reminded of God's grace and how sufficient it is in the time of need. Looking back, the treasure I learned here is from 2 Corinthians 9:8, **"And God is able to make all grace abound toward you; that ye, always having all sufficiency in all things, may abound to every good work."**

God had allowed me to be able to think clearly again so that I could intercede and guide Marie in making the right decision about her breast cancer. This is what I call grace, though I did not realize it at the time. God's grace gave us everything we needed to make the right decisions regarding Marie's care. Not only was it sufficient, but it produced a good work that brought glory to God.

Although my recovery phase was interrupted by Marie's illness, by God's grace I started to unwind and relax. I was able to rest, pray, and commune more with Him throughout the day with a clearer mind. I still had joint, muscle, and body aches with fatigue, but I was improving. However, the fatigue would not diminish right away. No matter how much rest I had, it just took time to leave my system. Though I could no longer feel God's presence, by reading His Word, I knew He was there and was seeing us through yet another storm.

Then my husband preached on John 17. As he delivered the message, I discovered that Jesus is talking to our heavenly Father in this passage. Jesus starts out praying for the disciples to know the only true God and Him, whom God had sent. He prays, *"That they may know you, the only true God, and Jesus Christ, whom you have sent"* (John 17:3 NIV). Jesus then goes on to pray for those who *will believe* on Him in the future, and my husband said that Jesus is praying for us here! Hearing this made me realize Jesus had prayed for me—little me. What a revelation to know that Jesus had prayed for me and all believers to be one with Him and the Father. *"That all of them may be one, Father, just as you are in me and I am in you. May they also may in us so that the world may believe that you have sent me"* (John 17:21 NIV). This truth brought such comfort to my mind, body, and soul—to know that Jesus desires such communion with me. He wants me to know the Father through Him—and with the intimacy that I too so desire.

I thanked God for my husband's sermon on this Scripture and started to pray this prayer to God, to make me one with Him through His Son, Jesus Christ, and to make me one with

Jesus, so others would come to know the Father. I knew the Scripture that I had recited over and over again in Philippians 3:10 was coming true. I wanted to know Him and the power of His resurrection, and the fellowship of His sufferings. I was truly overjoyed that God was answering my prayer.

My walk with God before these events was a walk in which I would *first* see and *then* trust God. But now He was showing me that even though I could not see my healing yet, or the healing of my sisters—or even if I no longer felt His presence—I was to trust that He was there and working everything out. I was gaining the assurance that I could know God on a deeper level through living by my faith in Him and not by my sight, feelings, or emotions. I was truly doing what the Bible said in Romans 1:17, *"The just shall live by faith."* I was becoming less independent and more dependent on God for everything, like my health, my family's health, and my finances—for all that concerns me.

God had taken us through the financial storm of our lives; my salary had dropped to half of what I had been making, and we had just bought a new house. But God was faithful to keep us in our home and provide for all of our needs. I was learning that He is *Jehovah-Jireh*—the God who supplies all our needs. I went from being an independent, self-reliant, and self-sufficient person to being totally dependent on God—in just one year's time. Moreover, I was starting to be a better person for it.

My recovery phase started out stormy, with Marie's diagnosis and my questioning God. But through those months, God was faithful. I reflected on the fact that there were now three of us diagnosed with breast cancer, and Jay had been stricken with a heart attack. God was opening up my understanding to know that I really could transfer all my fears, anxieties, and worries onto Jesus. As a result, I was learning how to go through the storms of life with Him.

The biggest treasure I learned in darkness was to: *Transfer everything to God and keep nothing.* My girlfriend Esther sent me a card with a Scripture that spoke to my situation: *"Cast all your anxiety on him because he cares for you"* (1 Peter 5:7 NIV). This message was truly a blessing for me and confirmed what God was already showing me.

Treasure

God is in charge of our lives, if we surrender to Him. We are to give everything to Him that comes our way and hold on to nothing. Remember; it had to come through Him first before it got to you.

RECONSTRUCTION: "I'M A NEW CREATION"

F our weeks after Marie's surgery, I went in for my reconstruction. On the advice of my oncologist, Dr. Lusch, the plan of having reconstruction done on the left side only had changed. With all three of us having breast cancer, he thought it was best to remove my other breast. My sisters and I were to be tested for the genetic mutation for breast and ovarian cancer, but the results would not be back before my surgery. So I took all of the doctor's recommendations and had my uterus, my ovaries, and my other breast removed to reduce the risk of recurrent breast cancer and possibly ovarian cancer. After what I had been through, I never wanted another menstrual period. Furthermore, my husband and I had decided not to have children.

I did not realize it at the time, but it was by God's grace that I had been gaining weight and went from size 8 to size 12. I had been so disgusted with the added weight that I had joined our women's weight-loss support group, but somehow I could not lose the weight. Later I found out that my weight gain was a blessing in disguise. Since I had gained so much weight, particularly in my lower abdomen, I had enough belly fat to have a TRAM Flap procedure. This procedure is done to make new breasts for a person who has undergone or will undergo a mastectomy. The surgeon uses the abdominal muscles and sometimes the fatty tissue of the lower abdomen, where women gain the most weight; and through surgery, the muscle and tissue is transferred to the upper chest. As an added benefit, I could also get an abdominoplasty, commonly called a "tummy tuck." The reason a tummy tuck is performed along with the TRAM Flap is that the adipose, or fatty tissue, in the lower abdomen overlies the muscles that will be needed to create the new breasts. When my plastic surgeon suggested this, I praised God. Although I could not figure out why I had gained all that weight following my chemotherapy, God knew what He was doing.

Another treasure I learned in the darkness is: *God was working all things out for my good. As the Scripture says in Romans 8:28, "And we know that all things work together for good to them that love God, to them who are the called according to his purpose."* God used the weight that I had gained to my advantage by allowing reconstructive surgery to make my new breasts and to also reap additional benefits for me. As the late Rev. William G. Henry, one of our associate ministers, used to say, "God is good all the time, and all the time God is good!"

In the preoperative holding area, while I was waiting to go back to surgery for my reconstruction, my husband, being the rock he is, kept me in stitches by telling me jokes. I'm not sure where he gets these jokes; but I guess he remembered when I had the mastectomy, I told him I was afraid that I was not going to make it. So, he must have stored them up just in case I needed them. However, this time I was not afraid. Finally, I could absolutely rest on God's promises, secrets, and the treasures He had already revealed to me through this dark period of my life. So, I was ready for my reconstruction—to get a new me—new breasts and a much-desired tummy tuck.

Before the surgery, I told the plastic surgeon to give me the best tummy tuck he had ever done. He did just that, and I could not stand straight for four weeks! The surgery took eight hours. I was pretty dazed by the narcotics, but I heard the nurse say, "They can't straighten her out because the doctor said she has a tight tummy tuck." I realized they were talking about me, and I said, "Way to go!" I was so delighted and grateful for finally reaching the end of my treatments.

The surgery went well, but the postoperative pain was very intense. I had never experienced that kind of pain before. Moreover, I had a reaction to almost every pain medication they gave me to relieve it. With every treatment or therapy I was getting for breast cancer, I began to realize what my patients were going through. This was going to be no different. For the many patients on whom I had performed hysterectomies, removal of ovaries, and even cesarean sections, I asked myself, *Is this the kind of pain they experience after their surgeries? Is this what they were talking about when they reported pain?* I vowed that I would never waste time talking with another patient when they were in pain; I would get them relief immediately!

The only thing that worked as pain relief for me was a morphine pump; however, I could not stay on that too long because it could cause other complications. All of the oral pain relievers made me sick. So by the end of the week, I had given up. I told Barb, who had come for my surgery, that God was working on me. I had been putting my faith in a team of doctors, and I was now going to put my faith back where it belonged. Even though I could not see my healing, I was going to start believing God for it, as I had done with Marie. Even if God did not relieve the pain, I was going to praise Him anyway. I then prayed and asked God for His comfort and strength to endure the pain.

Needless to say, I was being a typical doctor by dictating my own medical care from the hospital bed. I told my surgeon that I was sure I had developed a bowel obstruction, since my bowels were not working. And on postoperative day five I continued to have extreme pain. I had to constantly remind myself that my healing was going to come from God and that I was not supposed to put my faith in anything that I could see. I told the Lord that whether He healed me or not, I was going to glorify Him right there in that hospital bed. I asked Him to forgive me for putting my faith in anyone but Him.

I started witnessing to my roommate and her family, and I found out that her daughter had just lost her teenager in a freak accident in England. Every day God would give me encouraging words for her. By the fifth day, they moved me to a private room because my roommate had developed an infection.

However, I also knew that it was to give the nurses some rest since not only was I dictating my care, but I was also dictating my roommate's care by telling them what she needed.

The treasure I learned here is: *Never put your faith and trust in man, regardless of that person's position in life (see Jeremiah 17:5). Only God is able to supply all your needs according to His riches in glory by Christ Jesus (see Philippians 4:19).* As soon as I recognized this truth, my surgeon walked in and said, "I think I have a drug that will work for you." Oh, I was learning how to surrender my life in every area, knowing that all healing comes from God. Although God was using the natural means to heal me through medicine, it was very clear to me that my healing was from Him.

I know that God is a God of mercy because once again I had found myself thinking about medicine and had reverted back to my medical training. I used to believe that if I could come up with the correct diagnosis and medicine my patients would be healed. Not so anymore. God had brought me to an understanding where I would now involve Him from the start in the patient's care. Through prayer and waiting on God, I would ask Him what He thought was appropriate for each patient, and then act accordingly. To this day, my patients know that I am a praying doctor and will seek God for answers regarding their illnesses. I will always keep before me the truth of God's Word. Psalm 103:3 (NIV) affirms that it is God who *"heals all your diseases."* And in Exodus 15:26 (NIV) God declares, *"For I am the LORD, who heals you."* Therefore, I believe it to be so—not only for me—but for my patients too.

On the seventh postoperative day, I left the hospital after

having a right mastectomy, bilateral breast reconstruction with a TRAM Flap, a total abdominal hysterectomy, bilateral oophorectomy, and a tummy tuck. This means that my right breast was removed, reconstruction was done to make my two new breasts through the TRAM Flap, the tummy tuck helped to make the new breasts, and my uterus and ovaries were removed in the process. I was truly grateful to God for getting me through this surgery and I had also learned the treasure: *God is the source of my strength and healing.*

Treasure

God is the only One who will never disappoint you. We must put all our faith in Him and not in man. The Word of God even says it: "Cursed is the one who trusts in man, who depends on flesh for his strength and whose heart turns away from the LORD" (Jeremiah 17:5 NIV).

HEALING PHASE: "IT'S ALL ABOUT A BROKEN LEG"

After all my treatments were over and my reconstruction was complete, I needed time to heal physically and emotionally. I had always told my patients there were two parts to healing: a physical part and an emotional part. As life would have it, I was going to live through this experience too. While the obvious need is to take care of the physical problems, such as fibroids, endometriosis, irregular bleeding, and so on, I also believe in attending to a patient's emotional needs as well. Due to the nature of an illness, a strong emotional component goes along with it that is directly related to the manner in which the illness disrupts an individual's life.

Some people are able to adequately handle the emotional

aspect and go on with their lives; but in other cases, depending on the severity of the illness, the duration of it, and the amount of havoc it caused, I would give that patient time off for emotional healing. Sometimes I would even recommend therapy. Typically, if I did not address the emotional aspect of the disease, I observed that these same patients would periodically come back with other problems. And often it was because the emotional impact of the initial problem had not been completely resolved.

At this point in my own life, I was being faced with what I knew to be true. I was healed physically—but emotionally I was a wreck. My mind and emotions were all over the place, and most of the time, I felt very helpless and gloomy. It always seemed as though a cloud of darkness would follow me throughout the day, as if it were a rainy and cold day outside even when the sun was shining. I could not shake this mood of doom and gloom. I would think, *What if my cancer comes back? What if I don't make it five years?* The "what-if" would drive my mind crazy.

After about a month of this, I realized that I was experiencing severe depression. I had suffered from depression at other times but was able to shake myself out of it, as I had done when Shereene and Marie were diagnosed with breast cancer. But this time I would pray, read the Bible, and meditate on God's promises—but to no avail. I was sinking deeply into a depressed state. Although I was eating, my sleep habits were poor. I could not fall asleep at night for hours on end, and when I finally did, it was almost morning.

My thoughts were filled with fear about my future of ever

practicing medicine again. I worried that I would not fully remember any of my medical knowledge. I lost interest in things I used to love to do, like walking Ramsey in the woods, and reading my favorite books by such authors as Bunny Wilson and Elizabeth George. Even my Sunday school lessons were a chore for me to do because of my lack of interest. I knew these were further signs indicating that I was suffering from depression. I figured it could be an emotional or chemical imbalance as to why I was depressed, but either way I sensed this was depression.

Finally, settling down with time to reflect over the past year, I thought about what all I had gone through with the three of us developing breast cancer, Jay having a heart attack, and our having to put Dad in a nursing home. This was yet another reason why I was distressed. We had always said that we would never put our parents into a nursing home. But after Marie was diagnosed with breast cancer, Mom returned to Philadelphia to help with her recovery. Dad could not stay in the house by himself, and he was in no shape to travel with her. However, Mom was able to find the most wonderful nursing home in Florida. It looked like the Ritz Carlton; the place was so clean you could almost eat off the floors. The staff was very attentive and nice to Dad, and when Mom returned to take him out, he said he wanted to stay there.

Considering all of these events, I was feeling extremely sorry for myself and sat down to have a pity party. Furthermore, I had a chance to really look at myself in the mirror, and I looked quite different than I did before breast cancer. I wondered about things like, *Will my husband still find me attractive?*

Will my hair and nails ever grow again? Will my breasts be lopsided forever? I had a new body, but it was not like the one I was used to. And although I loved my tummy tuck, I just looked very different. When I told my husband that I might be depressed, he marched me straight to a Christian therapist. I told Roland, "I don't need therapy. Do you think I'm crazy?" He explained to me that I had all the signs, and there had been enough for me to be depressed about. He put on his pastor's hat and said, "You are going."

With that, I knew he was right. In addition to having difficulty sleeping, there were other signs, such as a preoccupation with what I had been through, and the feelings of hopelessness about my future. I had to admit that these signs indicated that I was suffering from depression. I figured it could either be from an emotional or a chemical cause, but either way, I was depressed. After all, I had every reason to be depressed, and I knew that I could not take care of patients in this condition. Therefore, off to the therapist I went. I was truly living out everything I had told my patients about what can occur after a major illness—you can get depressed.

When my husband told me that I needed therapy, somewhat reluctantly I obeyed and went. I wanted to work, but I knew that I was not really ready. However, my disability insurance carrier was threatening to discontinue my payments. They said I should have been ready to return to work by then, in spite of my depression and the fact that I was still suffering from extreme fatigue with muscle and body aches. My doctor agreed that I was not ready and wrote letters confirming my condition. Nevertheless, I felt pressured to return to work and guilt-ridden because I was still having problems. I constantly worried about this and thought, *Why can't I be like the patients who could return to work sooner than I can, and some who could even work during their treatments?*

I was informed that there would be a hearing in June and that I would receive a decision by July or August about whether my compensation would be discontinued. So, I convinced myself that I needed to get better—and soon. I was in therapy at the time, but my husband told me that God has the final say. He advised me that I was not ready to do the work of an OB/GYN due to the demand it would place on my physical and emotional health. He said to leave this in God's hands because God knew my condition, and that I should wait and pray.

I took his sound advice and thought to myself, *If God can shut up the mouths of lions in the book of Daniel and make a king have a dream in the book of Esther so that Mordecai would be saved from death, can He not represent me in the hearings?* I waited and prayed. Every month, I received my check and continued in my treatments to get better. God eventually worked this situation out in His own timing. It was not until the following January, when my therapist said that I no longer needed treatment that I heard from the disability administration a month later. By then, I had been healed emotionally, and I told them that I was ready to start looking for a job.

The treasure I learned here is: **God is faithful. *"Faithful is he that calleth you, who also will do it" (1 Thessalonians 5:24).*** I needed to stay on the course God chose for me, which was to get healed emotionally. This was confirmed by my husband /pastor and Dr. Lusch. God took care of the finances for me to do so. He never let them cut off my disability until I was healed. It was nothing that I did; I didn't call to complain that they were really mean to me, or even write letters indicating that I thought they were being unfair. I allowed God to fight my battle—and He won.

As I was going through that period of depression, my eldest brother, James, would call daily to check on me. For several months he would talk to me on a regular basis. James would give me updates on my niece Michelle; she was doing great in high school and played in the school band. She was also becoming fluent in Japanese and seriously studying Japanese culture. He was proud of her accomplishments, and so was I. Although he did not know that I was depressed, I knew God was using him to help me fight depression.

My therapist worked with me for ten months, twice per month. I did not take any medicine, but God used him to speak encouraging words and to provide the emotional healing that I so desperately needed. He took me back to my childhood and explored our family dynamics. I began to realize that I was an overachiever and was driven by the praise of men—instead of the praise of God. I was trying to please my family, and I sought after perfection in order to get this praise. After I developed breast cancer, I was out of work; I was financially dependent upon others and was not achieving anything academically. As a perfectionist, to me this meant that I had let my family down by getting breast cancer.

He helped me to see that I really needed an emotional healing. Through this therapy, I found out why I let my breast lump keep growing without going to see a doctor. I really wanted to be off this roller coaster on which I had put myself, but I could not let my family, my job, or my patients down by stopping to get treated. As an overachiever and a perfectionist, this would be viewed as being a failure on my part. Neither of these two characteristics will allow you to stop and think about yourself, much less stop and take care of yourself.

I also realized that I had been suffering from depression long before I had developed breast cancer, due to the constant pursuit of perfection in which I found myself. I was doomed for failure since I could not keep up with the standards I had set for myself; neither could I maintain the kind of relationship I desired to have with God. I felt so guilty if I missed my devotion time and prayer. My therapist pointed out that the guilt was making me depressed because God was also on my list of those whom I must please. And I simply could not forgive myself for letting both God and me down. This godly man was able to show me that the cross of Jesus Christ paid everything for me and that I did not need to earn God's approval; I only needed to rest and abide in Him. He assured me that God wanted me to do my best—but not at the expense of trying to add anything to the cross! Furthermore, I was already a believer in the Son of God, and I did not need to earn my way to heaven. The discovery of this truth was truly an enlightening experience for me.

God also used my husband's sermons to speak directly to me. He kept preaching that it was an abiding relationship with Jesus that was important. He taught that we could not keep the law (for me, that meant being a perfectionist) because then we would not need Jesus. My husband/pastor stressed the importance of abiding with Jesus, resting in Him, and surrendering one's life to Him. This truth spoke to my heart when I realized that God would do the rest as I surrendered to the Holy Spirit's control over my life.

I tell you, this was the breakthrough for me that revolutionized my entire thinking about being a Christian. As I learned to surrender every part of my life to God—medicine, healing, finances, and relationships—the more peaceful I became. I am no longer driven by the art of perfection, but by the Holy Spirit who guides me. During those months, I continued in prayer and daily communion with God, learning how to practice being in His presence—whether I felt that He was with me or not. By faith, I knew He was there. Through reading the book of Psalms, I discovered that others also suffered from depression. As I studied the Psalms, I noticed that the cure came through *praising* and *communing* with God, who is our Savior and deliverer. For example, reading and meditating on Psalm 42 brings out this point; it really blessed my life.

Over time, my depression started to lift as I continued to meditate on the Psalms. Others were praying for me, and I began to pray for others. This made me focus less on myself; I gave up the pity party and became glad that I was alive and that God had healed me. My desire for intimacy with God began to intensify, just as it had before my journey with cancer began. Now I welcomed this intimacy with a renewed sense of true desire to have a genuine fellowship with Him and not a relationship driven by guilt or obligation. My life became like a tree that was blossoming in the spring.

After ten months of counseling, I felt that I was finally and completely healed—both physically and emotionally. Now I could identify with the words Jesus spoke to the woman with the issue of blood, *"Your faith has made you whole"* (Matthew 9:22, paraphrased). I was finally there. I finished with my counseling that January and was feeling great. I had gained a much more positive outlook on the future, realizing my medical knowledge had not been lost. I could read my Sunday school lessons with enthusiasm and also enjoy my Christian books. I looked forward to waking up in the morning to see what God had planned for me. Even though it was in the dead of the winter with snow on the ground, I could walk Ramsey again; I was so thrilled that I wanted to walk. The treasure I learned here is: **God is faithful to His Word.**

I felt then that it was time for me to look for a job. As I started to search, my husband thought I was not quite ready yet. He said, "Give yourself a few more months without having any treatments, and then you will be ready." He reasoned that I had just finished counseling, which is also considered treatment, and that I needed more time to rest without any type of treatment activity going on. I thought to myself, *Oh, no, but I want to work and get back to a normal life.* Naturally, he left the final decision up to me. I was determined to show him that I was ready, so I went out on interviews.

I was even ready for a second interview with a company when one day I was out for my favorite pastime of walking Ramsey in the snow-covered woods. My neighbor stopped his truck to speak to me. And as I turned to catch my dog from jumping at his truck, I suddenly heard a crack at my ankle. I went down on the ice like a ton of bricks! In a matter of seconds, I had broken my leg and was screaming at the top of my lungs because of the excruciating pain that I was feeling. My neighbor had to pick me up and put me in his brand-new truck. Ramsey, my overprotective rottweiler, would not leave my side, so he had to put him next to me in the backseat. He had just bought that truck!

He raced down the hill and banged on our front door. My husband came rushing frantically to answer the door and saw me screaming in the car. Ramsey jumped out of the car and headed toward my husband. When Ramsey was secure in the house, my neighbor picked me up and handed me off to my husband, saying how sorry he was. Roland asked, "What happened?" My neighbor told him the whole story, and then we all realized he was standing there in his undies. So my neighbor left immediately. My husband quickly dressed and took me to the emergency room. Of course, this all happened on the Sunday morning of his pastoral anniversary!

Needless to say, I could not attend. After taking me to the hospital, I was diagnosed with a broken leg, which was placed in a temporary cast. Roland had just enough time to hurry to church and arrive in time to preach the sermon. One of my church members told me that she knew something was going on because when he sat down in the pulpit, she could see that he was wearing Timberland boots with his suit and no socks.

To my chagrin, I needed surgery and was laid up for five weeks—with no interviews, no nothing. I learned another treasure in darkness: *It is better to listen to my husband and submit to him as the Bible says in Ephesians 5:22: "Wives, submit yourselves unto your own husbands, as unto the Lord."*

Once again God was speaking directly to me through

Roland's prompting that I was not ready to go back to work quite yet. But this time I did not fall into a state of depression by focusing on myself or having a pity party. Rather, I took it in stride and asked God to comfort me as I rested and prayed. I quoted and meditated on Romans 8:28, *"And we know that all things work together for good to them that love God, to them who are the called according to his purpose."* This Scripture was a constant reminder that I needed God to turn this out for my good.

My recuperation time allowed me to surround myself with opportunities for God to minister to me in different ways. I read Brother Lawrence's book, *The Practice of the Presence of God.* I had more time for reading the Bible, and I started reading my favorite devotionals again, such as *Streams in the Desert* by L. B. Cowman and *My Utmost for His Highest* by Oswald Chambers. I also enjoyed watching Trinity Broadcasting Network, which airs some of my preferred television pastors. I loved hearing the teaching and sermons of David Jeremiah, Charles Stanley, Tony Evans, and James Kennedy—just to name a few. When I could walk again, I helped out at the after-school program at our church. Altogether, this time became a very enriching experience for me.

My husband was a good sport, and we did not dare call my mother again to nurse me back to health. He waited on me hand and foot. God bless his soul. I am also extremely grateful for the women of my church. Some of them came over one evening to fellowship with me, and it was a blessing. Over great food, we had prayer and devotions, and they sang songs. God bless them. My spirit was lifted, and I knew that God had sent them.

By the end of the spring, my cast was off. However, I did not rush into looking for a job. Instead, I asked my husband what he thought was best for me. He said, "Look, but spend more time in prayer rather than in looking." He told me to ask God to open the door where He wanted me—not where I wanted to be. Until I had the encounter with the sick lady during my chemotherapy treatment, I had decided that I really did not want to do full-time work. I didn't want direct patient care anymore, but instead I wanted to work for an industry, like a pharmaceutical company. After that situation, I was willing to go back to medicine—but still on my own terms.

My husband did not think that I should give up direct patient care. So, with the broken leg, I had learned my lesson. As I prayed specifically for a job, I said, "Not my will, but Your will be done, Lord." I knew my life was no longer my own, and I was going to live a life surrendered to God. I sincerely meant that He could send me anywhere He wanted and that I would go. Surprisingly, God only opened the door for me to practice full-time gynecology with my previous boss in Philadelphia. I knew that this was God speaking to me when my boss called. I took the job without hesitation, and I thanked God and my husband.

So now, after I was healed physically and emotionally, which incidentally took about two and a half years, I went back to work with a renewed sense of who God really is. I had learned to seek healing directly from the Word of God, which means that I practiced God's presence every day—in spite of whether I felt that He was there or not. I was no longer depending on myself or trying to be self-sufficient in anything. All of my sufficiency rests in Him. I had stopped trying to be perfect to win man's approval, but I rested in my Savior, Jesus Christ, who paid for all my sins on the cross. I was no longer guided by my emotions or feelings, but by the Word of God and the Holy Spirit. I would no longer dictate to God what I thought He should do for me. And I decided that I would take care of my health at all costs. I learned that God heals both supernaturally and through natural means. God decides which way He heals—and if He chooses to heal. I would now openly display this truth to my patients.

My therapist had cautioned me that, when I went back to work, there had to be balance in my life. In order for me to have peace, my priorities would be: God first, my family, my church, and then my job. The stress of being perfect had to rest with the cross; therefore, I could now live and enjoy my life resting in all that I know about my Savior. Dr. Charles Stanley, a great Bible teacher, explains how we should acknowledge that we cannot handle this life in our own strength; rather, we must submit to the Savior to make things right, and believe by faith that He can and He will do it. I wholeheartedly agree with this teaching because I am a witness that it truly works.

By God's grace, I worked two years at my job, and then God saw fit to bring me home to write this book. The work was good, but I found myself feeling fatigued, driving the one-hour-and-fifteen-minute commute each way in heavy traffic to Philadelphia. But this time the commute was sweet since I had learned how to commune with God throughout the day. In spite of unpleasant circumstances, I have learned how to be in constant fellowship with God and to see everything as coming from Him. Therefore, situations don't seem so bad now that I know He is able to see me through whatever He places in my path. Speaking of this, my dog, Ramsey, died from cancer in the midst of my writing this book. I am deeply saddened because I feel like I have lost my best friend. However, I'm depending on God for even the little things in life now, and I'm grateful for the time I had with Ramsey. He was truly a trouper throughout my illness. During the first seven to ten days of my chemotherapy, Ramsey never left my side.

It has been five years since my diagnosis and treatments, and by His power, I am still alive and healed. Not only was I healed physically through the medicine that God ordained and used to heal me—even though God knows that I did not want to be healed that way—but He also gave me a spiritual healing of my mind and soul. Through counseling, God used that situation of depression I went through to heal the emotional aspect of my illness, which so many people ignore. And through this trial, my mind and body were healed, and my soul rested well in Him.

I was like the woman with the issue of blood, who was so desperate to be healed that she reached out through the crowd to touch the hem of Jesus' garment. Jesus turned to her and, because of her faith, He said, "Woman, your faith has made you whole" (see Matthew 9:22). I too am made whole—not because of anything I deserve—but because of my newfound faith in the ability of Jesus to heal my mind, body, and soul. My desperation in reaching out to form an intimate relationship with Him has caused me to be completely healed. This is God working by His amazing power. The treasure I learned here is: *When you submit to God and His plan, it then becomes God's timing to open the door to implement His plan.*

I may be speaking to one woman or many women, those with a lump or who suspect they may have a lump. I hope my story has been an encouragement for you to go and seek treatment now. If you have delayed getting an exam because of fear or other reasons, it is never too late. As you can see from my situation, God is able to see you through—no matter how long you have waited—*go and seek treatment.* We are never too far beyond getting help and treatment because God has the final say. You should contact your primary doctor or gynecologist if you suspect a breast mass or lump—and see them promptly. They will refer you to the appropriate specialist to obtain breast imaging studies as needed. But the key is to go and get treatment, and believe God can—if it is His will and desire—heal you through natural medicine. Believe in faith that He has the power, and leave the rest up to Him. And be aware that your whole body, mind, and soul need to be healed as well—and only Jesus can do that.

You are not a failure any more than I was. Some women do not need to get counseling, and that is a blessing. But where there is a major illness, most of the time it is going to affect your mind. Depending on how it affects you personally, you may need therapy or medicine to get your mind in alignment with the same healing as your body. The two go hand in hand. The key is to recognize that you may need psychological counseling and then get it. The mind is also an organ of the body, and it is just as important as the heart, lungs, kidneys, and so on. When they get sick, you get treatment for them, do you not?

Remember that God is interested in a complete healing process. So the spiritual side to the healing of your body also involves your mind and soul—as all are healed by God. When the three are in unison, it brings sweet joy to you and all those around you. The healing of the body, mind, and soul can *only* be done by Him and through Him. God says, "Not by might, or by power, but by My Spirit" (Zechariah 4:6). Total healing comes as a result of reaching out to Him through prayer, meditating on His Word, and allowing Him to quietly heal you through the indwelling of His Holy Spirit in your body, mind, and soul—so that you too are made whole.

Treasure

God and only God is able to heal. He may use natural or supernatural means, but the bottom line is that healing comes from God (Psalm 103:3). It is His decision whom He heals, when He heals, and how He heals. If God heals you supernaturally and only you know about it, recognize that God did it, and praise Him greatly for that. But mostly He heals, I believe, through the natural by using medicine and doctors. However, I learned it ultimately comes through by His ordained authority, and God is to get the praise, not the doctors or the medicine.

CONCLUSION:
"SECRETS
AND TREASURES"

For two and a half years, I battled breast cancer. To put it succinctly, it was the most challenging and difficult period in my life. But I must say that all of the treatments and suffering that I endured in that darkness during my breast cancer storm pale in comparison to the secrets and treasures that my Lord and Savior, Jesus Christ, taught me. You see, God had placed a desire within me to know Him in a more intimate way, but I had to learn how to be in this kind of relationship with Him. Through the ordeal of having breast cancer, God taught me that such intimacy could only come through daily communion and fellowship with Him. Moreover, my journey through the storm uncovered the priceless treasures that showed me the path to victory in achieving that much-desired goal. Through it all, I believe this was the most valuable treasure that I learned.

Through trying to cope with the busy life of an OB/GYN and a first lady, I began to realize that I was in a seemingly endless rat race. It took me some time to figure this part out, but I also noticed that God was not in that race. I had been trying to box Him into only a portion of my life, that of my devotion time. However, when God allowed my circumstances to change by finding out that I had breast cancer, He showed me how to quiet myself and make major adjustments in my schedule so that I could have this great fellowship with Him.

Although I did not know it at the time that I started this journey, I eventually discovered that God had been with me the entire time. As I went through the steps to be cured of cancer, I learned how to reach out to Him throughout my day and to develop a strong personal bond of dependence on God that I know will last throughout my entire lifetime. When I no longer tried to limit my experience with God to times that I had set aside for my devotions, I was learning to depend on Him, which made all the difference in the world to me. I am truly convinced that this is one of the greatest treasures a Christian can know about God. It is a secret that is well worth finding out.

Through this experience I have learned the art of surrender. It became clear to me that God has the final say in our lives, if we submit all to Him. I discovered that the more I surrendered to God during this ordeal, the more He showed me the direction in which I was to go. But to do this requires obedience; the more obedient I was to God in surrendering to His way, the more He guided me in His will. This was all new to me. Before this journey, I was an independent thinker even though I had been a Christian for several years. My life was not really one of surrender to God; rather, I depended on my own means to achieve success. I did not know that He is a God who is able to lead and guide and that He wants to do a mighty work through each of His children. But during this journey of being healed of breast cancer, I learned the steps to surrender, and it turned out for my good.

You must come to the realization that you cannot do anything apart from Him. Jesus said, *"Apart from me you can do nothing"* (John 15:5 NIV). Recognize this truth and continually step aside so the Holy Spirit can do His perfect work within you. I found that the hardest part was the stepping aside, because it seemed easier to go after what I want, to work out all the details, and then ask God to bless my plans. But the only way I could step aside was when I was flat on my back and my hands were tied with breast cancer—that is when I saw God's mighty power working for me.

What this means is we must continually discipline ourselves to think like a child and know our heavenly Father can work out our circumstances without our help. It is the constant renewal of our minds by the Word of God through reading and meditating on it to see how He worked in the lives of others. Then we must believe that He can and will do the same for us when we desire His will to be done and not our own. This may be difficult because it goes against our nature, but if we are born again we have a new nature that can and will submit to God—if we step aside.

The stepping aside is as simple as saying, "Lord, I don't

know what is best for me in this life, so I'm going to depend on You to show me the direction to go." Act as if your hands are tied all the time and see how God works. You must enter the kingdom as a little child; a child knows his mother will feed and clothe him and he does nothing to assist or help her. God works in the same way as we submit to Him; He will come in and assist us and never let us down.

Through the practice of relying on the Lord for my daily needs, I became more disciplined because I had to keep my focus on God. Now I have an inner peace and my spirit is more tranquil. I can see things from God's perspective, and not my own. I have the kind of peace that the prophet Isaiah talked about when he said, *"Thou wilt keep him in perfect peace, whose mind is stayed on thee: because he trusteth in thee"* (Isaiah 26:3). Discovering this treasure brings about a constant state of peace. As a result, my life is now more peaceful, and I can rest on His promises to see me through whatever comes my way.

I found that the secret to staying focused on God is achieved through worshiping Him. I learned how to worship God in a way that not only occurs while I am in church; now worshiping God throughout each day, hour, or minute is essential to my very being. I really appreciate Oswald Chambers's comment on this truth, "A private relationship of worshiping God is the greatest essential of spiritual firmness."[1] This is one of the greatest treasures I can pass on to you. Reach out to Him in whatever state you are in and start to worship, fellowship, and commune with Him. Then you will see what God will do for you. Try it for thirty days, and you will never be the same.

I must tell you another secret—God is in charge of your life, just as He is mine. And each individual has unique experiences designed by Him. So if you need healing, you should know that you cannot dictate to God how you want to be healed and think He is going to obey your command. I thought I had a benign breast mass and kept asking God to remove it supernaturally so I would not need to interrupt my busy schedule to have treatments. I'm sure a lot of this was even denial and the fear that it could have been cancer and not wanting to face the truth. But God did not adhere to my command because He is not to be dictated to. He is God, and I am not; neither are you.

God also taught me that I was not so indispensable and essential to His plan that I could not get sick. He showed me this and even had mercy on me, not to allow my tumor to progress past my lymph nodes before I finally surrendered and sought treatment. Subsequently, my delay in getting treated probably caused me to have a more intense storm. It forced me to experience almost all of the treatments that breast cancer patients have to endure. But by His grace, He saw me through this storm. Because of His mercy, He did not chastise me and make me suffer longer than I needed to; I could have even died from advanced cancer, but God did not allow this to happen.

Through this adversity, I realized what true grace and mercy are, and I will never dictate to God again about how I am to be healed. And I will seek treatment immediately when I am ill. I will always remember how He kept me during the trial of it all. I can now assure you that His grace and mercy are able to see you through each and every storm in your life, if you call on Him and surrender your life to Him. Second Corinthians 12:9 brought me comfort, and it will also comfort you because of

God's promise, *"My grace is sufficient for thee: for my strength is made perfect in weakness."*

In whatever present state you may find yourself, even in the midst of confusion, I pray that God will show you how to rely on your faith in Him to bring you out of it. God wants you to stop and wait on Him to show you His direction and which path to take. The way to make decisions in life that will honor God is to place your trust in Him to lead you to victory over your situation. This tells us and the world that we serve an all-powerful God who is able to cause us to triumph over the hard times in life.

When I was diagnosed and had utter confusion as to where I should go for my treatments, I finally stopped and acknowledged that God knows everything and that I did not know what to do. If I could figure it out, it would probably be wrong anyway. So what was I to do? I acknowledged God's presence and gave Him control of my life. Then God stepped right in and directed my path to where I needed to go. To my own amazement, I learned to trust that He is the supreme God by stopping and waiting on Him to direct my steps—and He led me to succeed over my adversity. Now I can share with others what I personally know to be true about the goodness of God.

There is another very important secret about God of which you must be aware; that is—you do not get to choose your troubles; God does. But you can trust in His ability to see you through anything He places in your path. The breast cancer was not of my own doing; I did not cause myself to get cancer. By delaying my diagnosis, I probably intensified my storm, which may have led me to need more treatments. But I did not cause my hardship. God allows us to go through adversities that help us to depend on Him so that we can get to know Him and experience His mighty power. God can and does reveal Himself to us in this way. During this time, He even showed me the true meaning of Philippians 4:13 when I learned that I could do all things through Christ who strengthens me. There were days when I did not think I was going to make it, but His strength saw me through.

I also observed in the storm that there is a tendency for people to curse God by asking Him the question, "Why me?" and then they turn away from Him. But I learned instead that we need to turn to God and find out what God is trying to say to us through difficult times. I say, don't waste time in a storm by not getting to know the Savior who can guide you out. It takes having faith in God to believe that He truly makes all things work together for our good as the apostle Paul reminds us in Romans 8:28. Therefore, I know by my faith in God that the journey that He took me through was a process that has ultimately worked out for my good. And as a result, God deserves all the glory.

All the secrets and treasures about His surpassing greatness that I learned about Him were worth my trial and the walk of faith that He guided me through. But I could not have learned these treasures about God's power if I could have walked by sight. It doesn't take faith to see something in order to believe it is true. It does take faith to believe God before the outcome can be seen. This treasure that is now stored in me would have never been there if God did not teach me to have faith in Him as He worked a miracle in my life.

My healing did not come in a supernatural manner, which I so desired. Rather, God healed me through natural means, and God did get His glory. If God had healed me through supernatural means, the scores of people with whom I came in contact during my treatments; the testimony that I was able to give about God's goodness, grace, mercy; and my new revelation of His healing power through the use of natural medicine would have never been the same. It is also possible that many would not have believed me if He had done it supernaturally. So, yes, as a doctor, I learned that God and only God is the healer, and as a result, I am a better doctor for my patients.

As I bring the story of my journey through breast cancer to a conclusion, I would not trade this experience for the world and would go through it all over again to learn these secrets and treasures of my Lord and Savior, Jesus Christ. I prayed that I would "know Him" based on Philippians 3:10. God answered that prayer, though not the way I would have chosen. Yet He turned it out for my good. I had known Him as the Savior of my life, but now I can truly say that He is my Lord as well. By this, I mean that I submitted my life to Jesus and He has complete control over it.

I hope that I have showed you the ups and downs in the life of an individual who has cancer. You can be so strong in the Lord one day, and the next day wonder how you made it through. One day I would be walking in grace, and then I'd get a cancer scare and fall from grace by falling apart. But this taught me to totally submit to God and rely on His will for me. Some may call this brokenness, but whatever you may call it, I can now say that God is in control of my life. I trust Him, I

adore Him, I've learned how to fellowship with Him throughout the day, and I'm totally dependent on Him. I love to be in
daily communion with my Lord and Savior. From what I have
learned, I am a better wife, doctor, Christian, and overall person
—because God gave me the desire of my heart—that I might
know Him. I thank God that now I can also agree with the
apostle Paul when he said in Philippians 3:8 that he would
give up everything to know the surpassing knowledge of Jesus
Christ. Yes, I can agree with that too.

1. Oswald Chambers, My Utmost for His Highest, updated ed., (Grand
Rapids: Discovery House, 1992) "Missionary Weapons," September 10.

GLOSSARY

benign: No cancer is found; noncancerous; not malignant.

breast: The breast is composed of two major tissues, glands and ducts. The glands are called lobules. The lobules are composed of breast milk. The ducts are vessels that provide the passageway for the breast milk to the nipple. The breast is also composed of fatty and connective tissue, blood vessels, and lymph nodes.

breast aspiration: A small needle used to enter the breast to remove fluid and cells if the breast mass is fluid-filled, or remove cells if the mass is solid. It is sent to pathology for evaluation for cancer, if necessary.

breast cancer: The abnormal growth of cells in the breast, arising mostly from either the ducts or lobules (glands). These abnormal cells have unconrolled growth that result in cancerous tumors. There are three major types of breast cancer: ductul arising from the ducts, lobular arising from the lobules, and inflammatory—a very aggressive form of breast cancer. There are other forms of breast cancer that are less common. Breast cancer can and does occur in men, though at a much lower rate than women.

breast carcinoma in situ: Cancer that has not spread beyond the original tissue of the breast; for example, it is in either the lobules or ducts and does not invade the surrounding tissue.

breast cyst: A fluid-filled mass in the breast that is benign, usually round, mobile, and tender.

breast implants: Artificial material shaped in the form of breasts and used in place of breasts when they are removed due to breast cancer. There are two major types: silicone or saline. Despite some controversy with silicone, they are still widely used today and appear to be safe.

breast lump: A mass of breast tissue that has formulated in the form of a palpable mass felt on physical exam.

breast mass: The same as a breast lump; but includes the possibility of the tissue only being seen on imaging studies and not necessarily palpable on exam.

breast prosthesis: Artificial material shaped in the formation of a breast to be used in the place of the breast for women who choose not to have breast reconstructive surgery.

breast reconstruction: A surgical procedure designed to produce new breast tissue after removal of the breast. There are several types; the TRAM Flap is just one type, but is the most popular.

breast surgeon: A doctor specializing in taking care of breast diseases who can perform surgery.

breast ultrasound: An imaging study with ultrasonic beams placed on the breast to evaluate a breast mass or abnormality. Mostly used to determine if a breast mass is fluid-filled (cystic) or solid.

centimeters: The metric system used to measure the size of a breast mass or lump and to measure the depth of invasion of the cancer cells.

chemotherapy: Destruction of tumor cells by cytotoxic medicine; given by IV therapy to kill the tumor as well as cancer cells that may be in other organs of the body.

fibroadenoma: A solid breast mass that is firm, solid, and mobile. It is a benign mass, usually slow growing, and may or may not be associated with pain.

fibrocystic changes: A benign condition of the breast that involves cystic areas (fluid-filled sacs) and fibrous changes (scar or connective tissue). It can lead to a lump formation and cause painful and swollen breasts.

gynecologist: A doctor specializing in taking care of the female reproductive system.

invasive breast carcinoma: Cancer that has spread beyond the capsule of the original tissue such as the duct or lobule into the other surrounding breast tissue.

lumpectomy: Removal of only the diseased breast tissue and surrounding area adjacent to the cancerous tissue.

malignant: Cancer is found.

mammogram: A radiologic study to image the breast. It can pick up early cancers that may not be detected by a physical exam.

mastectomy: The complete removal of the breast.

medical oncologist: A doctor who specializes in taking care of cancer patients.

metastatic breast cancer: Cancer that has spread beyond the breast to other areas of the body, such as the bone, liver, brain, etc.

MRI: An imaging study used to image several areas of the body; can be used to image the breast and can detect tumors not seen by a mammogram, in particular, very early breast masses.

oophorectomy: Removal of the ovaries.

preoperative chemotherapy: Chemotherapy given before the surgery, which can shrink the tumor prior to its removal.

plastic surgeon: A doctor who specializes in reconstructive and reparative surgery.

postoperative chemotherapy: Chemotherapy given after surgical removal of the cancer.

radiation oncologist: A doctor who specializes in giving radiation therapy to cancer patients.

radiation therapy: A form of treatment using radiation (radioactive particles) to destroy cancer cells.

radiologist: A doctor who specializes in performing radiologic procedures and reading imaging studies.

solid breast mass: A lump that is solid and has no fluid-filled areas or cysts. It can cause tenderness and should be evaluated by a surgeon.

total abdominal hysterectomy: Removal of the uterus and cervix through the abdomen.

TRAM Flap: The abdominal muscle that comes from the upper abdomen is transferred to the breast area to make new breasts for breast reconstruction.

tummy tuck: An abdominal procedure that removes the fatty tissue from the lower abdomen to enhance a woman's waist-line. It is done with the TRAM Flap to help create new breasts during the breast reconstruction.

◆
AFTERWORD

You may ask what a person can do to help fight the cause for a breast cancer cure. There are several things that will greatly help. You can volunteer your time to a breast cancer foundation that helps patients by providing transportation to appointments, making telephone calls for encouragement, doing grocery shopping, and running other errands. You can donate funds to the breast cancer societies in your local area or to the national foundations. When I developed cancer, my sister Marie bought breast cancer awareness postage. By making these purchases, a portion of the proceeds is donated to support research. It can be that simple. If you don't have a lot of time or money, just the small cost of buying stamps will help.

You can also pray for cancer patients in your church and community or form an outreach program or support group to provide comfort. Also remember to pray for and support the family members of cancer patients; they need care too.

The following resources may be helpful to you for more information or to volunteer your support:

Breast Cancer Societies:

The American Cancer Society
800-227-2345
www.cancer.org

Linda Creed Breast Cancer Foundation
1601 Walnut Street, Suite 1418
Philadelphia, PA 19102
215-564-3700
www.lindacreed.org
Donna Duncan, Executive director

Living Beyond Breast Cancer
888-753-5222
www.lbbc.org

National Cancer Institute
800-422-6237
www.cancer.gov

Rise Sister Rise Breast Cancer Foundation
Zora Kramer Brown, Founder
202-463-8040

Sisters Network, Inc
866-781-1808
www.sistersnetworkinc.org

Susan G. Komen Breast Cancer Foundation
800-462-9273
www.komen.org

Women of Faith and Hope
P.O. Box 14228
Philadelphia, PA 19138
215-849-7004
Novella K. Lyons, Executive Director
www.wofah.org

Y-Me National Breast Cancer Foundation
800-221-2141
www.y-me.org

ISBN 0-8024-8989-3
ISBN-13 978-0-8024-8989-0

This practical, encouraging and biblically-based manual will help trauma survivors —and their loved ones—move toward healing. Philadelphia-based, licensed psychologist Collins describes how trauma victims get caught in the trauma zone, a place they want to escape but can't. Some can't move forward, feeling stuck and victimized by their past. Some can't see, living in denial of what has happened. And others can't learn from the past, repeating the same mistakes over and over. All of them find they can't cope with the overwhelming emotions that accompany trauma. Dr. Collins believes there is a way out of the trauma zone and back to emotional health, a path he outlines in this practical, encouraging book.

by Dr. R. Dandridge Collins

Find it now at your favorite local or online bookstore.

www.LiftEveryVoiceBooks.com

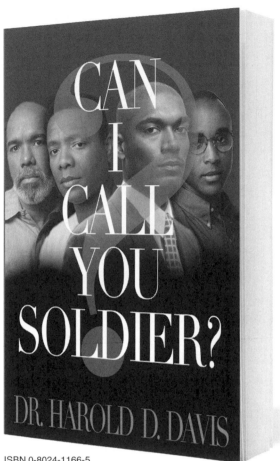

ISBN 0-8024-1166-5
ISBN-13 978-0-8024-1166-2

A generation is under attack…who will protect your family?

The war is at home and the battlefield is in the lives of our young men. In any community, and particularly in the black community, millions of young men feel the void of a role model. For every absent father, complacent leader, and passive bystander, there is someone who will step in and fill the father figure void—whether he is a trustworthy man of God or a dangerous enemy. It's up to us to win this battle and prepare the next generation to join the fight.

by Dr. Harold D. Davis
Find it now at your favorite local or online bookstore.
www.LiftEveryVoiceBooks.com

LIFT EVERY VOICE

Can *Two* Walk *Together?*

Encouragement for Spiritually Unbalanced Marriages

Sabrina D. Black

ISBN: 0-8024-1771-X
ISBN-13: 978-0-8024-1771-8

A wonderful tool to provide those in unequally yoked relationships the hope and help they need to deal with disappointment and heartache. Sabrina Black assists couples with creating and maintaining a vibrant, growing relationship despite their spiritual differences.

by Sabrina D. Black
Find it now at your favorite local or online bookstore.
www.LiftEveryVoiceBooks.com

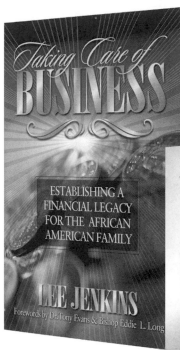

ISBN 0-8024-4016-9
ISBN-13 978-0-8024-4016-7

Available
September
2007

ISBN 0-8024-8801-3
ISBN-13 978-0-8024-8801-5

Lee Jenkins offers readers comprehensive strategies for setting goals in the areas of family, faith, friends, finances and fitness. These goals will transform the hearts and then the lives of people who want to improve their financial situation.

Strengthen your future. Empower your family. Improve your finances. These are the ministry goals of Lee Jenkins, registered investment advisor, financial speaker, and author of Taking Care of Business. He answers the most common questions he is asked at his financial conferences, combining biblical wisdom, financial deftness, empathy and encouragement in this powerful guide.

by Lee Jenkins
Find it now at your favorite local or online bookstore.

www.LiftEveryVoiceBooks.com

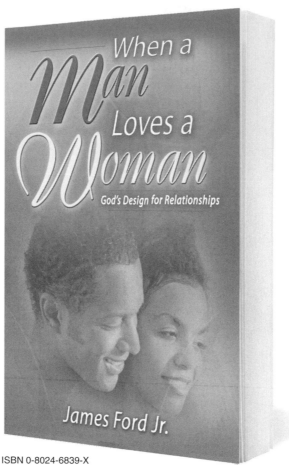

ISBN 0-8024-6839-X
ISBN-13 978-0-8024-6839-0

"Everyone knows that Jacob of the Old Testament was a rascal, a usurper, a deceiver. But Jacob knew how to love a woman. If you want to know if a man really loves a woman, take a close look at what Jacob has to tell us." Pastor Ford takes a look at Jacob's lasting love for his wife, Rachel, gleaning insights on how men can meet the social, emotional and spiritual needs of their wives.

by Pastor James Ford, Jr.
Find it now at your favorite local or online bookstore.
www.LiftEveryVoiceBooks.com

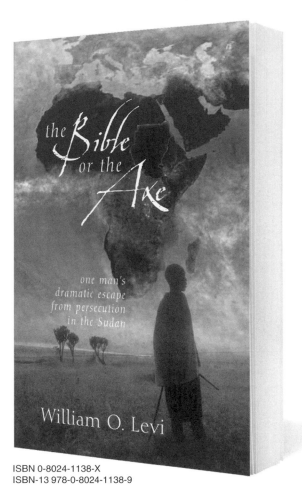

ISBN 0-8024-1138-X
ISBN-13 978-0-8024-1138-9

On the banks of the muddy Kulo-jobi River, a young Sudanese boy is face with a decision that will shape the rest of his life. Read the riveting, true story of one man's escape from the Sudan, and how he later came to help his people.

by William O. Levi
Find it now at your favorite local or online bookstore.

www.LiftEveryVoiceBooks.com

The Negro National Anthem

Lift every voice and sing
Till earth and heaven ring,
Ring with the harmonies of Liberty;
Let our rejoicing rise
High as the listening skies,
Let it resound loud as the rolling sea.
Sing a song full of the faith that the dark past has taught us,
Sing a song full of the hope that the present has brought us,
Facing the rising sun of our new day begun
Let us march on till victory is won.

So begins the Black National Anthem, written by James Weldon Johnson in 1900. Lift Every Voice is the name of the joint imprint of The Institute for Black Family Development and Moody Publishers.

Our vision is to advance the cause of Christ through publishing African-American Christians who educate, edify, and disciple Christians in the church community through quality books written for African Americans.

Since 1988, the Institute for Black Family Development, a 501(c)(3) nonprofit Christian organization, has been providing training and technical assistance for churches and Christian organizations. The Institute for Black Family Development's goal is to become a premier trainer in leadership development, management, and strategic planning for pastors, ministers, volunteers, executives, and key staff members of churches and Christian organizations. To learn more about The Institute for Black Family Development, write us at:

The Institute for Black Family Development
15151 Faust
Detroit, MI 48223

We hope you enjoy this book from Moody Publishers. Our goal is to provide high-quality, thought-provoking books and products that connect truth to your real needs and challenges. For more information on other books and products written and produced from a biblical perspective, go to www.moodypublishers.com or write to:

Moody Publishers/LEV
820 N. LaSalle Boulevard
Chicago, IL 60610
www.moodypublishers.com